THE RUSSIAN REVOLUTION, 1917

uncovered editions

Series editor: Tim Coates

Other titles in the series

uncovered editions

THE RUSSIAN REVOLUTION, 1917

∘◦⊰⊱◦∘

London: The Stationery Office

Applications for reproduction should be made in writing to the
Contracts and Rights Manager, The Stationery Office Limited,
St Crispins, Duke Street, Norwich NR3 1PD.

Second impression 2000

ISBN 0 11 702424 4

First published 1919, 1921
© Crown copyright

A CIP catalogue record for this book is available from the
British Library.

Typeset by J&L Composition Ltd, Filey, North Yorkshire.

Printed in the United Kingdom for The Stationery Office by
Biddles Ltd, Guildford, Surrey.
TJ3110   C10   12/00

Uncovered Editions are historic official papers which have not previously been available in a popular form. The series has been created directly from the archive of The Stationery Office in London, and the books have been chosen for the quality of their story-telling. Some subjects are familiar, but others are less well known. Each is a moment of history.

Series editor: Tim Coates

Tim Coates studied at University College, Oxford and at the University of Stirling. After working in the theatre for a number of years, he took up bookselling and became managing director, firstly of Sherratt and Hughes bookshops, and then of Waterstone's. He is known for his support for foreign literature, particularly from the Czech Republic. The idea for "Uncovered Editions" came while searching through the bookshelves of his late father-in-law, Air Commodore Patrick Cave OBE. He is married to Bridget Cave, has two sons, and lives in London.

In World War I (1914–18), Britain, France and Serbia were allied with Russia against Germany, Austria and Turkey. Fighting on the Eastern front caused far greater loss of life even than in the battlefields of France.

Socialism as an idea for a new form of government in which far greater numbers of people benefited from the wealth of nations had been developing for many years. In Russia several groups had been working for the overthrow of the Tsarist regime, which they saw as corrupt, evil and self-serving. These groups saw socialism as an international movement. It was their intention that people in all countries should benefit from the upheaval of capitalist and monarchist governments.

The British government, along with most governments of wealthy powerful nations, watched the rise of socialism with suspicion and uncertainty. In some circles it was a fashionable idea and a possible development of the liberal attitudes of the beginning of the new century, but more entrenched capitalists took a much more hostile view.

The Russian Revolution of 1917 broke out in the midst of the most terrible war. The British Parliament endeavoured to monitor and analyse its progress by gathering such information as it could from British citizens who became caught up in the awful developments. They published these reports without comment, in order to provide a first-hand description of what was happening.

The opening pages of this book are an extract from a Foreign Office review of the nature of the Revolution. The second part contains the verbatim account of those who could get their reports out of the country.

Note: spellings have been retained as they appeared in the original papers.

PART ONE

∞⚬✕⚬∞

Events leading up to the Russian Revolution in February 1917 and how the Bolsheviks came to power in October 1917

[Extracts from the Report of the Committee to Collect Information on Russia. Cmd 1240, 1921]

Russian Revolution

0
500 Miles
0
500 Kilometres
Arctic Ocean
Novaya Zemlya
Norwegian Sea
MURMANSK
ARCHANGEL
VLADIVOSTOCK
Sea of Japan
Sweden
Finland
Norway
STOCKHOLM
KRONSTADT
PETROGRAD
NIJNI NOVGOROD
PSKOV
VERKHOTURIE
PERM
TOBOLSK
KAMISHLOF
EKATERINBURG
MOSCOW
KAZAN
SARANSK
Russian Federation
Estonia
Latvia
Lithuania
Denmark
COPENHAGEN
Belorussia
TULA
OREL
KURSK
WARSAW
Germany
Poland
Czech Rep.
Slovakia
Ukraine
OMSK
Kazakhstan
Austria
Hungary
Romania
Moldavia
ODESSA
Yugoslavia
Bulgaria
BLACK SEA
TASHKENT
Uzbekistan
Greece
Turkey
CHITRAL
Afghanistan

∞⚬⚭⚬∞

Influence of the war on Lenin

THE outbreak of war in August 1914 threw the
Socialist parties throughout the world into confusion.
The resolutions adopted against war and providing
for international strike action in the event of the outbreak of war remained dead letters and entirely
without effect. A great stream of the population in
the various belligerent countries flowed into the war,
and not only were the official leaders of the Socialist
parties powerless to fight against this, but in a large
number of cases they abandoned their opposition to

capitalist government and gave their wholehearted support to the war.

The Russian Social Democratic Labour Party suffered no less than others from the effects of the crisis. Alexinsky, formerly one of the "Vperedovtsy," or "Forwards," the extreme wing of the Bolsheviks, left the Bolshevik group and joined the so-called Social patriots. Plekhanov, who had for so long been associated with the Bolsheviks, and especially with Lenin, also stood out for the war.

Lenin, alone, stood firm. In the autumn of 1914 he published his thesis on the war. He pointed out that the European war had definitely assumed a character of a bourgeois, Imperialist war; its sole, real purpose was to plunder countries and to fight for markets. Its tendency was to befool, disunite and murder the proletariat of all countries in the interests of the bourgeoisie.

He censured the conduct of the leaders of the German, Belgian and French Social Democrats, who had voted for war, as treachery to Socialism and the spiritual bankruptcy of the Second International. He professed to see the cause of this in the predominant influence of petty opportunism in the International and declared the task of the future International to be the irrevocable and decisive emancipation of Socialism from bourgeois influence.

Turning to the situation in Russia, Lenin stated that the task of the Russian social democracy was merciless and unconditional struggle against the Great Russian and "Tsarist–monarchical–chauvinism," and against the efforts of the Russian Liberal Intellectuals to defend it. He therefore defined the programme of the Russian social democracy as follows:—

1. Widespread propaganda advocating Socialist revolution among the troops, and especially at the front, emphasising the necessity of directing their weapons not against their brothers, "the hired slaves of other countries," but against the reactionary bourgeois Government and parties in all countries. Hence it became necessary to organise illegal groups among the troops of all nations for the purpose of disseminating propaganda in all languages. Besides this, there must be a merciless struggle against the chauvinism and patriotism of the bourgeois and petty bourgeois of all countries. He appealed to the revolutionary conscience of the working masses who bore on their shoulders the whole burden of the war, against the leaders who had betrayed Socialism.

2. Republican propaganda, advocating the establishment of republican forms of government throughout Europe.

It has been said that the war impelled Lenin further towards the Left, away from a more central position which he formerly adopted in the Bolshevik section of the Russian Social Democratic Labour Party.

It would, in our opinion, be truer to say, not that his views swung further to the Left, but that his attitude towards the possibility of realising his views in practice underwent a change with the war and made him feel that the outbreak of the European struggle, promising physical and economic suffering proportionate to the wide area over which it was waged would bring revolution nearer in one or other, perhaps in all, belligerent countries.

Thus, while bitterly opposing the war and the mutual extermination of the proletariat in the interest of the bourgeois classes, he gradually began to calculate the possibilities of overthrowing capitalist society on a basis of the proletarian suffering which the war would bring about. It was not, therefore, that the war occasioned any fundamental change in Lenin's views. It was only that as the war went on, and widespread suffering was caused and extended more and more, that his ideas passed from the realm of shadowy political speculation to that of ideas whose realisation the morrow might see.

At a conference of foreign sections of the Russian Social Democratic Labour Party, held in March 1915 at Berne, on his own initiative, Lenin further developed his attitude to the war, and declared the necessity for establishing the Third International, which he was to succeed in doing exactly four years later in Russia.

In September of that year, he was present at the International Conference of Socialists opposed to the war held at Zimmerwald, where he advocated the publication of a manifesto urging the necessity of bringing the war to an end and replacing it with civil war in the various belligerent countries.

In the following year he was present at a Second Internationalist Conference held at Kienthal, where he bitterly attacked the Mensheviks for the support they had given to the war. In answer to this attack, Martov, representing the Mensheviks of the Left, presented to the conference a declaration of the Petrograd Menshevik workers, censoring the Social patriots and even those who had consented to serve on the War Industry Committee established in connection with the war. On this occasion Lenin, supported by Radek and Rosa Luxemburg, proposed to the conference that a policy of general strikes, sabotage and armed revolt should be resorted to for the purpose of bringing the war to an end.

∘◦⊰⊱◦∘

Causes leading up to the Revolution

WE now proceed to consider the position in Russia towards the end of 1916, and to outline a series of factors which contributed collectively to demoralise the Russian army, to undermine the economic structure of the State, to discredit the autocracy, and thus create that atmosphere of despondency, despair and apprehension which prevailed throughout Russia in the month of February 1917.

The course of the war showed:—

1. That Russian industry, still in a relatively primitive

stage of development, could not supply the technical equipment necessary to make a large army a potential fighting factor under conditions of modern war.

2. That the Administration was corrupt and inefficient, and ill-suited to concentrate, adapt and develop the resources of the country for the successful prosecution of the war.

3. That great numbers of men were mobilised indiscriminately, without regard to the maintenance of enterprises essential to the State both at home and at the front, or to the possibility of training and equipping those who were called up. Thus, in 1916, there were thousands of unemployed soldiers in Petrograd and other centres, who, while as yet unaccustomed to army discipline, were left idle in the barracks.

4. That, in a special degree, the railway services suffered (*a*) serious depletion, both of their experienced administrative staff and skilled mechanics; (*b*) owing to the transformation of certain railway repair shops into factories for the preparation of munitions.

This occasioned a decline in the efficiency of the railway services, which ultimately became progressive. It was evident in 1916 that the transport system was no longer able adequately to maintain, at one and the same time, the supply of the armies at the front and of the population at home.

This state of affairs reflected very seriously on the operations of the army. The failure to supply sufficient heavy artillery, machine guns, rifles and ammunitions exposed the army to enormous losses at the hands of an enemy admirably equipped with the most powerful and deadly weapons of modern war.

Moreover, the shortcomings observed in the Government at home were repeated in the administration of the army, and in the handling of forces in the field. Absence among the officers of moral leadership over their men and deficiency of military knowledge, more especially among junior officers, and in the more highly technical branches of the service, were revealed as time went on. There was, moreover, an absence of sympathy among the officers for their men, which in many cases gave rise to bitter feeling against the officers among the rank and file.

A statement of the losses of the Russian army from August 1914 until February 1917 is essential to an understanding of the situation both in the army and in the country, immediately prior to the revolution.

The casualties of the army in the first ten months of the war are said to have been 3,800,000, and a Russian staff officer has estimated the total losses up to the beginning of the revolution at 10,000,000, and expressed the opinion that the army had had to be replaced three times entirely along the whole front of 700 miles during the period August 1914 to January 1917.

These colossal losses created an extraordinary impression throughout the army. In addition to the incompetence and disorganisation everywhere prevailing, it was suggested that treachery was also active, and that forces were at work at the Court whose object it was to promote the defeat and dissolution of the army with a view to making inevitable the conclusion of a separate peace between Russia and the Central Powers. By the autumn of 1916 a large number of officers and the majority of the intelligentsia—patriotic, active and resolute—had been led to the conviction that a state of affairs had arisen which could not be allowed to go on.

It has been said that, eighteen months before the revolution broke out, discipline in the army had begun to be affected as a result of the disorganisation both at the front and in the rear and the enormous casualties sustained, and that revolution became a common subject of discussion among the officers in the messes of the Guard Regiments.

The revelation, in the course of this year, of the scandals proceeding at the Court, and associated with the name of the Monk Rasputin, still further deepened popular resentment against the autocracy. The appointment of Shtürmer, a notorious pro-German, as Prime Minister in December 1916, was quickly followed by the murder of Rasputin. It is held by many that the revolution may be said to have begun with these events.

It was in these circumstances that the Duma met in February 1917. During this month blizzards interrupted railway traffic and the delivery of flour to Petrograd. The bread supply failed. Long queues were to be seen throughout the city, and in the working-class quarters bread was scarcely to be obtained at all. A series of mass demonstrations began. The bridges across the Neva were drawn up, but thousands of hungry men and women poured across the frozen river and made their way to the Nevsky Prospect on the other side.

On the morning of Monday, the 28th February/ 13th March, four Guard Regiments revolted, dis-armed their officers, and killed or arrested them. The revolution had begun.

February to October 1917. The rise and fall of the Provisional Government.

THE revolution was sudden, spontaneous and all-embracing. All classes of the population gave to it their active support or tacitly acquiesced in it. It was so sudden and unexpected that there were no signs of any premeditated plan of revolutionary action. The soldiers of the Petrograd garrison, ignoring or opposing the orders of their officers, flowed out on to the streets of Petrograd and joined the hungry crowds of workmen.

The Liberal members of the Duma, who had created the atmosphere in which the revolution broke out, found themselves taken unawares and were utterly powerless. The Provisional Committee of the Duma, which was formed during the political crisis preceding the revolution, was unable to restrain the forces which the revolution had released. The city was in the power of a mass movement, irresponsible, uncontrolled and uncontrollable.

On Tuesday, the 14th March, M. V. Rodzyanko, the president of the Provisional Committee of the Duma, proceeded to communicate by telephone with the staffs on the various fronts, and thus secured the adhesion of the officers throughout the army to the revolution. At the same time, the Soviet of Workers', Soldiers' and Peasants' Deputies was being formed upon the model of the Soviet of 1905, in the Tavrichesky Palace, where the Duma used to hold its sessions and where the Provisional Committee of the Duma was then sitting. The Provisional Committee represented, broadly speaking, the Liberal elements of the Intellectuals. The Soviet, on the other hand, represented the Russian Socialist movement.

On Wednesday, the 15th March, the Provisional Government was formed. The Executive Committee of the Soviet declined to put forward its candidates for posts in the Government, and confined itself to appointing a committee to act as an intermediary between the Soviet and the Provisional Government. A. F. Kerensky alone of the Socialists considered it his duty to enter the Government, and accepted the post of Minister of Justice.

It is important for the purpose of this report that the character of the Soviet, the atmosphere in which it worked and its attitude towards the Provisional Government should be clearly understood—in the first place, because the Soviet was regarded as the leader of the revolution by the workers and soldiers in Petrograd and by the rank and file of the army and the popular masses throughout Russia; second, because it was in the Soviet that the Bolsheviks were represented and in it that they came to play a more and more influential and ultimately a dominant rôle. The Provisional Committee of the Duma, on the other hand, loomed vaguely in the minds of the masses as a reactionary remnant of the old order which had passed away. The tide of revolutionary events swept over it and it soon became forgotten. The Provisional Government, to which it had given birth, inherited the popular suspicion with which it was regarded.

The Petrograd Soviet consisted of about 1,000 members, who were elected or appointed during and immediately after the revolution in a haphazard and indiscriminate manner from the military units of the Petrograd garrison and factories in and about the city. The Soviet appointed an Executive Committee of about 100 persons to transact current business and direct its work.

The Executive Committee in action at this period presented a picture of chaos. It sat daily from 1 o'clock, throughout the afternoon and night and often far into the morning. No rules of procedure had as yet been elaborated for it. The agenda was usually decided on the spot by the committee as a whole. At times not one of the questions which it was elected to discuss, were decided, and often irrelevant issues arose which diverted the attention of members from questions under discussion. The occasions upon which plenary sessions of the Soviet were held are described as affording an example of "catastrophic disorder."

Most of those who attended these turbulent assemblies were taking part in political life for the first time and many of them were half illiterate. Additional confusion was introduced into the activities of the Soviet, inasmuch as its individual members took occasion to act in the name of the Soviet on a number of questions, large and small, without consulting the Executive Committee and without its knowledge. M. Stankevich, a witness, concludes, with the following words, a graphic description of the conditions under which the Soviet conducts its work: "Most important decisions were taken often as a result of an entirely chance majority. There was no time to think, for everything was done in haste, after sleepless nights, and in confusion. Physical fatigue was general. Broken sleep, endless sessions, absence of regular meals, living on bread and tea, with sometimes a soldier's dinner eaten from messtins without knives and forks."

Friction between the Provisional Government and the Soviet immediately arose owing to the following reasons:—

(1.) The Soviet, while declining to participate in the Government and share its responsibilities, took executive action independently of the Provisional Government, notably in the case of the Soviet's famous Order No. 1, recommending the formation of Soldiers' Committees in the army.

(2.) The Soviet, showing an instinctive tendency, made inveterate by custom, to assume a negative attitude to the existing Government and, distrusting the Provisional Government as the representative of bourgeois interests, put forward a series of demands which were tantamount to reducing the authority of the Government to impotence. The Soviet made the following demands, among others: The substitution of militia, subordinated to organs of local self-government for the police, the retention of arms by the Petrograd garrison, and liberty—otherwise committees—in the army.

We now pass to the situation brought about by the revolution in the army.

It has been seen:—

(1.) That discipline was undermined in the army before the revolution, and that the rank and file were weary of war.

(2.) That the officers of the Russian army did not command as a whole the respect and

confidence of their men, and that a gulf was
thus created between them.

(3.) That a number of officers had begun to
regard revolution as inevitable if Russia was
to remain in the war and play an efficient
part in it.

It was in these circumstances that, in accordance
with the recommendations contained in Order No.
1, issued by the Petrograd Soviet, Soldiers'
Committees or Soviets sprang up throughout the
army. The complete absence of any plans governing
the formation and procedure of these committees
reproduced, on a far greater scale, the chaos which
has been described in the Petrograd Soviet and still
further increased the confusion which a change of
this fundamental character might be expected to
cause in the army.

Committees were everywhere formed on different lines, in some cases with officers and in others
without. The functions of the committees, their duties
and powers, and the methods by which they were
elected were invariably left to the discretion of each
particular committee itself.

The result of these disrupting influences was that
the army, upon which the Government relied to maintain the front against the enemy, and for support within
the country in the last resort, lost all cohesion and
became a source of danger to the Government itself.

The effect of the revolution in the countryside
was an almost universal tendency on the part of the

peasants to seize the estates of the landed gentry. In some cases, the landowners or their agents were killed or driven away. The lands of the Church were not exempt from this spontaneous and uncontrollable movement. Soviets of Peasants' Deputies sprang up in all parts of the country, and either began to exercise a dual power with the local representatives of the Provisional Government or took local affairs entirely into their own hands. The Zemstva (Boards of Local Self-Government) came to be looked on with suspicion and to lose their authority.

The eight months from February to October 1917 may be divided into three periods:—

The first period, February 28 to April
During these two months the Petrograd Soviet enjoyed enormous popularity and authority. Representatives of the army and provincial Soviets flocked to it from the front and from all parts of Russia, clamouring for direction and advice. The Petrograd Soviet was for this brief space of time the embodiment of the revolution. We have seen, however, that whatever opportunity this unique position might have given the Petrograd Soviet of becoming an organising and controlling authority in the revolutionary movement was destroyed by the chaos which confused its own counsels.

The second period, approximately from May to July
It was one of the ironies of the revolution that the Petrograd Soviet lost its popularity at the time when

its leaders had succeded in introducing into it those elements of organisation which were essential to any utilisation of the unique position in which it found itself after the outbreak of the February revolution. It was also at this time that the Soviet had come to realise the necessity of the participation of its representatives in the Provisional Government. The cause of this loss of popular confidence was the necessity under which the Soviet found itself of defining its attitude towards the European war. Whatever prestige the Provisional Government had had among the people melted away after the declaration of Milyukov, as Foreign Minister, supporting the acquisition of the Dardanelles by Russia on the successful conclusion of the war.

An unbridgeable gulf separated Milyukov's views from those expressed by the Soviet in its manifesto to the people of the world published on the 27th March. So strong was the tide of popular feeling in favour of the manifesto that the Provisional Government itself was compelled to state its preparedness to raise the question of peace without annexations and contributions in its diplomatic relations with Allied Governments. But, with the arrival of more and more grave news from the front with regard to the growing disorganisation of the army; with the arrival of foreign delegations of labour representatives, urging the necessity of the Russian army continuing to fight in the name of democracy for final victory over the Central Powers; with the necessity for representatives of the Soviets to participate in

the Provisional Government, unless they were prepared, as they were not, to assume the entire
responsibility for the Government of a disordered
country—a sudden change swept over the Petrograd
Soviet. This change was marked by the decision of the
Soviet, accompanied, however, by various reserva-
tions, to support the war. The result was that among
the troops in the Petrograd garrison, throughout the
army, and in all parts of Russia the Soviet lost popularity. The Soviet proceeded to send its representatives
to the front for the purpose of influencing the Army
Committees to persuade the soldiers to fight. While,
therefore, the relations between the Petrograd Soviet
and the Government, in spite of the change, cannot
be said to have undergone any material improvement,
the effect of the Soviet's support of the war and of the
entry of its members into the Provisional
Government identified it, in the mind of the masses,
with the Provisional Government as pursuing a policy which was opposed to the collective will of a
spiritually exhausted and physically wearied people.
Meanwhile the Bolsheviks had begun to play an
important part in the Soviet, and Trotsky, almost
immediately after his arrival from America, succeeded
in establishing an ascendency at its meetings by his
unbounded energy and fiery oratory.

The third period, July to October
The hopes which had been raised of an improvement
in the discipline of the army were dashed to the
ground by the failure of the June offensive. The

Bolsheviks, whose representatives had begun to appear on the Army Committees, upon the town Soviets and in the countryside, exploited the defeat to the utmost. They emphasised in their public utterances the inability of the army to fight further on behalf of a cause which they declared to be that of the class enemies of the proletariat and of the poor peasantry. Their prestige among the masses grew uninterruptedly, and, as the summer wore on, they began to develop more and more as a power in the Petrograd Soviet itself. The Provisional Government became a helpless figure-head. The misunderstanding between Kornilov and Kerensky finally discredited both the Government and those who saw the only hope of successfully opposing the Bolsheviks in the establishment of a military dictatorship. Amidst the divided counsels and mutual recriminations of those whose united action was essential to the stemming of the advancing tide the Provisional Government became a melancholy spectre of Governmental impotence. Alone among this babel of dissentient voices the cries of the Bolsheviks "Down with the War," "Peace and the Land" and "The Victory of the Exploited over the Exploiters" sounded a clear and certain note which went straight to the heart of the people.

In the course of October the Bolsheviks secured the majority of the Petrograd Soviet. In the first days of November a manifesto was issued by the Soviet signed by two Bolsheviks, Podvoisky and Antonov, calling upon the troops of the Petrograd garrison to rise to the support of the Soviet which the manifesto declared to be in danger. With this manifesto what is known as the October revolution may be said to have begun. For two or three days action on both sides was paralysed by fear and uncertainty. The Government were afraid to act because they felt the last shreds of power had slipped from them, the Bolsheviks because they could not bring themselves to believe that the Government were powerless to deal a counter-blow against them. Finally, however, they occupied the Government buildings one by one without opposition. The Provisional Government simply melted away.

PART TWO

∞⦾⦿⦾∞

Events from the summer of 1918 to April 1919

[Extracts from a Collection of Reports on
Bolshevism in Russia. Cmd 8, 1919]

The following collection of reports from His Majesty's official representatives in Russia, from other British subjects who have recently returned from that country, and from independent witnesses of various nationalities, covers the period of the Bolshevik régime from the summer of 1918 to April 1919. They are issued in accordance with a decision of the War Cabinet in January 1919. They are unaccompanied by anything in the nature either of comment or introduction, since they speak for themselves in the picture which they present of the principles and methods of Bolshevik rule, the appalling incidents by which it has been accompanied, the economic consequences which have flowed from it, and the almost incalculable misery which it has produced.

Sir M. Findlay to Mr. Balfour.—(Received August 20.)

(Telegraphic.)   *Christiania* [*Oslo*], *August* 19, 1918.
I HAVE received following telegram dated the 9th August from Woodhouse and Cromie at Petrograd to General Poole:—

"British subjects have been arrested during the past two days without any charge having been made against them, but only two have been detained so far. We protested and asked for explanation. On 5th August all British officials at Moscow were arrested, but the majority were subsequently released and are presumably now under house arrest.

"Their probable evacuation was notified to us, and we were warned to be ready to leave with them, but as yet we have no definite news from them. Commissary threatens to intern all allied subjects. Please inform London of above, as we are not allowed to telegraph in any direction. Tell London also that up to the present all are well here. In Petrograd position of Soviet Power is becoming rapidly untenable, and orders are being given for various units and places to be evacuated. That they are in touch with Germans is quite evident. A yacht is ready at Peterhof to take Lenin away."

Sir E. Howard to Mr. Balfour.—(Received August 20.)

(Telegraphic.)   *Stockholm, August* 19, 1918.

FOLLOWING is a summary of the more important points in a series of despatches from Mr. Wardrop, at Moscow:—

"*August* 5.—About 4.30 this morning a band of ten armed men attacked consulate-general and demanded admittance. Without my authority one of the inmates of the house opened the door, being threatened with fire-arms. This was the fourth armed raid on the premises.

"Guards left at 5.30 and local commissary expressed his regret at the incident.

"During the morning I learnt of arrest of several British subjects, including Messrs. Armitage,

Whitehead, William Cazalet Hastie (over seventy years old), North (chaplain), Beringer (Reuter's agent), and Miss H. Adams, one of my staff. In the afternoon, while Mr. Lockhart was calling, another raid on the premises was made with warrant for arrest of staff. I protested and declared that I only yielded to force. Office was sealed in great detail, seals being attached to every drawer, to both safes, and to all receptacles for papers, also to outer doors to the office rooms. All the staff were then arrested, including Mr. Stevens, Mr. Douglas, and lady clerks, and conveyed to Soviet's police quarters in Tverskoi Boulevard. Mr. Lockhart, Captain Hicks and I were not arrested, as Chicherin had promised that consuls and military missions should not be arrested. Their staffs, however, had not been specifically mentioned. French military attaché, General Lavergne, was liberated after short arrest. Staff were detained. Guards were stationed to watch my premises and I was left in my private apartments there. I do not regard failure to arrest myself and Mr. Lockhart as evidence of intention to treat us better than our staffs, but rather the contrary.

"I do not regard Bolshevik detention of our nationals as aimed at deterring us from vigorous action in distant places, so much as intended to protect Bolshevik leaders on their fall. They are converting houses in centre of the city into improvised fortresses in the belief that there will be soon a serious rising, in which their Allied prisoners will serve as centres. Finally, if they regard all as lost they will probably hound populace on to massacre these prisoners.

"*August 6.*—Consul Stevens, Vice-Consuls Lowdon and Douglas released about 3 A.M., also North and others, and French Consul-General Grenard and French Consul Labonne, by efforts of Swedish colleague who spent the night in negotiations.

"At 10 P. M. following still detained:—

"Vice-Consuls Wishaw, Greenep, and Jerram, passport officer Webster and his assistant, Ginson senior, Tamplin and Linger of Lockhart's staff, Fritz Mucukalv and the Misses Galbaly and Adams of my staff. Prisoners so far fairly comfortably housed and fed and allowed to associate with one another. Guards conciliatory.

"I am allowed to go in and out, and Mr. Lockhart and his remaining staff can visit me.

"*August 7.*—I called at temporary prison and saw Greenep, Wishaw, and Jerram. They are all well treated by their guards who are real Russians, unlike most of their leaders, who are either fanatics or Jewish adventurers like Trotsky or Radek.

"All British and French women are now released. Also Mr. Beringer and others.

"*August 8.*—Wishaw, Greenep, Jerram, and Webster brought here this morning by efforts of my Swedish colleague. Whole staff of consulate-general now at liberty.

"It is also suggested that during our stay at Petrograd we shall be under a Bolshevik guard. Evidently Bolsheviks are trying to prolong negotiations. City is on the whole quiet. All ex-officers under sixty are to report themselves this morning, probably with a view to their arrest, and there are rumours of wholesale arrest of clergy."

Sir R. Paget to Mr. Balfour.—(Received September 3.)

(Urgent.)

(Telegraphic.)   *Copenhagen, September* 3, 1918.

FOLLOWING report from Danish Minister at Petrograd has been communicated to me by Danish Government:—

"On 31st August the Government troops forced their way into the British Embassy, their entry to which was resisted by British naval attaché, Captain Cromie who, after having killed three soldiers, was himself shot.

"The archives were sacked, and everything was destroyed.

"Captain Cromie's corpse was treated in a horrible manner. Cross of St. George was taken from the body, and subsequently worn by one of the murderers.

"English clergyman was refused permission to repeat prayers over the body.

"French Military Mission was forced. A man named Mazon and a soldier and several Frenchmen were arrested.

"Bolsheviks in the press openly incite to murder British and French.

"It is urgently necessary that prompt and energetic steps be taken."

Sir R. Paget to Mr. Balfour.—(Received September 10.)

(Telegraphic.) *Copenhagen, September* 9, 1918.

I HAVE received telegram from Petrograd as follows:—

"Wholesale arrest and decapitations have resulted from attempt on Lenin and murder of Uritsky. Bolsheviks are arresting bourgeoisie, men, women, and children, having no connection with the authors of these attempts, on the plea that they are faced with conspirators.

"According to official reports, more than 500 persons have been shot during the last three days without enquiry or sentence. Fresh executions are being prepared, and the press is full of blood-thirsty articles.

"Lockhart was arrested and condemned to death, but at the last moment we succeeded in saving him; 28 British, including British consul, and 11 French have been arrested at Petrograd. In the prisons conditions defy description. In fortress of Peter and Paul, where all the British are confined, prisoners have absolutely no food. In order to remedy this, we have now succeeded in forming an organisation. Every night executions take place without trial. Terrorism continues. Protest against these proceedings has been made verbally and in writing by foreign representatives, including Germans. List of more than 1,000 hostages has been published by the Government, amongst whom are four Serbian officers, who will be shot if attempt on life of a commissary should be made."

Mr. Lindley to Mr. Balfour.—(Received September 11.)

(Telegraphic.)   *Archangel, September* 6, 1918.

I HAVE just received news of murder of Captain Cromie by Bolsheviks, and accusations of latter against him.

Fact is that gallant officer devoted his whole time at Petrograd to the service of his country. His first object was to prevent Baltic fleet falling into German hands; he then helped in evacuating valuable stores, and latterly gave most of his attention to plans for preventing a German advance on Vologda. These activities, carried out for months in daily danger of his life, brought him more or less into co-operation with Russians hostile to Bolshevik régime and therefore claimed as reactionaries.

His plans may very well have included destruction of certain bridges as Bolsheviks declare. In Captain Cromie, His Majesty has lost a most gallant, capable, and devoted servant.

Sir M. Findlay to Mr. Balfour.—(Received September 18.)

(Telegraphic.)   *Christiania, September* 17, 1918.

FOLLOWING is report by Netherlands Minister at Petrograd, the 6th September, received here to-day, on the situation in Russia, in particular as affecting British subjects and British interests under Minister's protection:—

"Sir—On 30th August I left for Moscow, largely in connection with negotiations for evacuation of

British subjects from Russia. The same day Uritski Commissary at Petrograd, for combating counter-revolution, was assassinated by a Jewish student Kanegiesser, whose father is a wealthy engineer and holds a very good position at Petrograd. This murder was at once attributed by the Bolshevik authorities and Bolshevik press (only existing press in Russia) to French and English.

"That same night Consul Woodhouse and Engineer-Commander Le Page were arrested at 1 A.M. in the street. Every effort was made the next day (31st August) by my secretary, M. van Niftrik, to obtain their release, and that of Consul Woodhouse was promised for the afternoon.

"At 5 P.M. on the 31st August, when Consul Bosanquet and Acting Vice-Consul Kimens, who had been busy the whole day with M. van Niftrik in connection with his attempt to obtain release of the arrested and were heading to the Embassy and were near the Embassy building, they were warned not to approach the Embassy, told that it had been occupied by Red Guards, and that two persons had been killed. They at once decided to head back to find M. van Niftrik and asked him to endeavour to secure entry into the Embassy. While driving slowly away from Embassy their car was stopped by Red Guards in another car, one of whom levelled a revolver at them and told them to hold up their hands. They were searched and had to give their names and rank, but to their great surprise were allowed to proceed. M. van Niftrik drove with them to Gorokhovaya 2, headquarters of the Commission for Combating Counter-Revolution, to which persons arrested are usually taken, and where Mr. Woodhouse was confined. He had a long interview with the commandant of Petrograd, Shatov, and strongly protested against the unheard of breach of International Law which had taken place, and demanded to be allowed to drive immediately to Embassy to be present at search there. Permission was refused by Shatov, who said that Embassy was being searched because authorities had documents proving conclusively that British Government was implicated in Uritski's murder. When they had left and their car was passing the Winter Palace, staff of British Consulate and of missions, and some civilians who were at Embassy when it was invaded, were seen walking under guard to No. 2 Gorokhovaya.

"A meeting of neutral diplomatic corps was held that night upon the initiative of M. van Niftrik, at which the following points were submitted:—

"1. That immediate release of those arrested should be demanded.

"2. That it should be insisted upon that M. van Niftrik should be present at examination of arrested.

"3. That attention should be drawn to gross breach of international law committed by armed occupation of the Embassy, which bore on the door a signed and sealed notice to the effect that it was under the protection of Netherlands Legation, and by refusal to allow M. van Niftrik to be present at the search.

"The meeting drew up a protest to be presented to the Soviet authorities at Moscow.

"On the 1st September particulars were learnt as to the violation of Embassy. The Red Guards, under the direction of several commissaries, had made their way into the Embassy at 5 P.M. and behaved with the greatest brutality. Captain Cromie, who had tried to bar their entrance, and had been threatened that he would be killed 'like a dog,' had fired killing two men. He had then been shot himself, and died nearly instantaneously. The whole staff of the Consulate and Missions and some civilians accidentally present at the Embassy, had then been marched under escort to Gorokhovaya No. 2, where they remained until Tuesday, the 3rd September, when (at 4 P.M.) they were conveyed to the fortress of Peter and Paul.

"During the next few days repeated efforts were made by M. van Niftrik, M. van der Pals, also Consul and neutral Legations to obtain release of those arrested, but without success. M. van Niftrik endeavoured successfully to obtain an interview with Zinovief, President of Northern Commune, on the 1st September; M. de Scavenius, Danish Minister, who expressed profound indignation at what had occurred, saw Zinovief at 9 P.M. on that day, and expressed himself in strongest terms. He was promised that body of Captain Cromie should be delivered up to him and M. van Niftrik, and on the 2nd September they together removed the body to the English Church. The funeral took place in the presence of the whole of the Corps Diplomatique and the greater part of the British and French communities. The coffin was covered with the Union Jack and was completely wreathed with flowers. After it had been lowered into the grave I pronounced following short address in French and English:—

> " 'In the name of the British Government and in the name of the family of Captain Cromie I thank you all, especially the representatives of the Allied and neutral countries, for the honour you have shown Captain Cromie.

> " 'Friends, we have all known Captain Cromie as a real friend, as a British gentleman, as a British officer in the highest sense of the word.

> " 'Happy is the country that produces sons like Captain Cromie.

> " 'Let his splendid and beautiful example lead us and inspire us all until the end of our days. Amen.'

"The doyen of the Corps Diplomatique, M. Odier, Swiss Minister, gave expression to his deep sympathy and admiration for the late Captain Cromie, who had died for his country.

"In the evening of the 3rd September, no impression having yet been made on the Communal authorities, another meeting of the Corps Diplomatique was held. This meeting was attended by neutral diplomatic representatives, and M. van der Pals, representing the Netherlands Legation. Unexpected feature of the meeting was the appearance of German and Austrian consuls-general. The

whole of the body met together at 9 P.M. and proceeded to Zinovief's residence, where they with
difficulty succeeded in obtaining an interview with
him. M. Odier strongly protested, in the name of the
neutral legations, at action taken by Communal
authorities against foreign subjects. He emphasised
the fact that for acts of violence committed against
foreign subjects in Russia the Soviet officials would
be held personally responsible. He demanded that
permission should be granted for a neutral representative to be present at the examination of the accused.
Zinovief said that he must consult his colleagues on
the matter. M. van der Pals afterwards again laid stress
on this point. M. Odier was followed by German
consul-general, who made a forcible protest in the
name of humanity against the terrorism now entered
upon by Bolsheviks. He referred in strong terms to
'sanguinary' speech of the other day by M. Zinovief,
and said that even though French and English
arrested belonged to nations at war with Germany,
yet it was impossible not to unite with neutral representatives in a strong protest against course now
adopted by Bolsheviks.

"I returned to Petrograd yesterday, as I had
received a telegram from my secretary urging my
return, and could not therefore take responsibility of
remaining longer absent from Petrograd, where position, I gathered, must be very bad. Up to today
situation here has in no way improved. Besides
British arrests, numerous arrests of French citizens
have taken place, including that of the commercial

attaché to French Embassy, though French consular officers have not so far been touched. Thousands of Russians, belonging to officer and wealthy classes, not excluding merchants and shopkeepers, are being arrested daily, and, according to an official communication, 500 of them have already been shot; amongst arrested there are a large number of women. For last four days no further British arrests have been made.

"Position of British subjects in prison is most precarious, and during last few days constant reports have reached Legation that question whether to shoot or release them has not yet been decided. There seems to be also a strong tendency to regard those arrested as hostages. Those belonging to military and naval missions are probably in most danger, and in present rabid temper of Bolsheviks anything is possible, but there is some hope that consular staff and civilians may be released before matters become still more serious. With regard to members of missions, hope of release seems very small.

"Conditions under which Englishmen at Peter and Paul fortress are kept are most miserable. I was informed yesterday by M. D'Arey, commercial attaché to French Embassy, just released, that they are crowded together with other prisoners, some twenty in a cell, twenty by ten feet. In each cell there is only one bed, rest must sleep on a stone floor. No food whatever is supplied by prison authorities, and they depend entirely on arrangements which this Legation had made and food furnished by friends and relatives.

Rugs, pillows, medicines, warm clothing, and other comforts are being sent from time to time, but great difficulties are experienced in getting these articles delivered. From the 31st August to morning of the 2nd September no food at all was accepted for prisoners. Since then they have received some supplied from outside, but it still remains to be seen whether it will reach them regularly at fortress, though I shall leave no stone unturned to secure its proper distribution. Russian prisoners in fortress appear to be absolutely starving, and this will make question of supply of British subjects even more difficult than it would otherwise be, owing to presence in their cells of famished Russians. I enclose herewith copy of letter just received from British prisoners, which speaks for itself.

"Yesterday evening I endeavoured to see Zinovief in order to inform him of appalling conditions at the fortress, but he absolutely refused to see me. I was equally unable to see Uritski's successor and could only gain access to a subordinate of latter, who behaved with lack of courtesy which may now be expected. I informed him of conditions obtaining in fortress, and he eventually promised to speak to commandant of fortress whom he had occasion to see that night. He refused to give me the number of Zinovief's telephone or name of commandant of fortress.

"As regards situation in Moscow, I can only say that in my opinion it is most grave. Nineteen Englishmen and thirty Frenchmen have been arrested and are kept under the worst conditions. Mr. Lockhart, who was released and subsequently re-arrested, was only saved from being shot on 4th September by my most strenuous exertions. Before I left Moscow a solemn promise was given to me that he would be released, but his position is precarious in the extreme, while all those now under arrest there are in great danger. Mr. Lockhart is accused by Soviet Government of organising a plot to overthrow it, and Bolshevik official and unofficial papers are full of details of alleged conspiracy, while it is asserted that British officials at Petrograd were concerned in plot. Attempt on life of Lenin is of course attributed by Bolsheviks to British and French, and if he should die it is quite possible that all now under arrest at Moscow and Petrograd would be shot.

"At Moscow I had repeated interviews with Chicherin and Karahan. Whole Soviet Government has sunk to the level of a criminal organisation. Bolsheviks realise that their game is up and have entered on a career of criminal madness. I repeatedly told Chicherin, with all the energy of which I am capable, that he must realise full well that Bolshevik Government was not a match for England. England had a longer wind than the Soviets. She would not be intimidated; even if hundreds of British subjects should be executed by order of the Bolsheviks England would not turn one hair's breadth from her purpose. Moment would come when the Soviet authorities, man by man, would have to pay for all the acts of terrorism which they committed. But in spite of persistence with which I drove those facts home, I could not obtain any definite promises from Chicherin but only a few evasive replies and some lies. Bolsheviks have burnt their boats and are now ready for any wickedness.

"As regards original objects of my journey to Moscow—evacuation of British from Russia—I found it necessary to promise that Litvinof should be allowed to leave England at once, provided that in exchange for this concession all British subjects in Russia, including consular staffs and missions, were allowed to leave the country. This was agreed to so far as consulates and civilians were concerned, including those now under arrest at Petrograd, but an exception was made with regard to members of military and naval missions, who would be released only on arrival of Russian Red Cross delegates in France for the purpose of repatriation of Russian soldiers. Result of negotiations was reported by telegraph to His Majesty's Minister at Stockholm for communication to British Government.

"As regards invasion of British Embassy at Petrograd, I had occasion to present to Chicherin and Karahan, in addition to my protest and demands for repatriation embodied in my note to Chicherin of 2nd September, joint protest drawn up by neutral diplomatic representatives at Petrograd (see above) which I also signed, demanding release of all those arrested at Embassy and that Embassy should be handed over to me, and stating that Soviet Government would be held responsible in every respect for consequences of this breach of international law which was quite unique in history. This I reported to my Government at The Hague, through the intermediary of Chicherin for transmission to British Legation there, though I cannot affirm that telegram was sent. Chicherin wished to evade question of release of persons arrested at Embassy, and only agreed to demand for Embassy to be handed over to me, but I told him plainly that it must be all or nothing, and that I would not consent to half measures of this kind. I have further demanded that all documents seized at the Embassy shall be delivered to me.

"The foregoing report will indicate the extremely critical nature of the present situation. The danger is now so great that I feel it my duty to call the attention of the British and all other Governments to the fact that if an end is not put to Bolshevism in Russia at once the civilisation of the whole world will be threatened. This is not an exaggeration, but a sober matter of fact; and the most unusual action of German and Austrian consuls-general, before referred to, in joining in protest of neutral legations appears to indicate that the danger is also being realised in German and Austrian quarters. I consider that the immediate suppression of Bolshevism is the greatest issue now before the world, not even excluding the war which is still raging, and unless, as above stated, Bolshevism is nipped in the bud immediately, it is bound to spread in one form or another over Europe and the whole world, as it is

organised and worked by Jews who have no nationality, and whose one object is to destroy for their own
ends the existing order of things. The only manner in
which this danger could be averted would be collective action on the part of all Powers.

"I am also of opinion that no support whatever
should be given to any other Socialistic party in
Russia, least of all to social revolutionaries, whose
policy it is at the moment to overthrow the
Bolsheviks, but whose aims in reality are the same,
viz., to establish proletariat rule through the world.
Social revolutionaries will never fight any foreign
Power, and any profession which they may now make
in this sense are merely a tactical move in their struggle with the Bolsheviks.

"I would beg that this report may be telegraphed
as soon as possible in cypher in full to the British
Foreign Office in view of its importance."

Following is copy of letter received from British
prisoners in the Fortress of Peter and Paul at
Petrograd, dated 5th September, 1918:—
"Your Excellency,

"We are not allowed to write letters. We will
write to you daily, since the chance of our letters getting through are very remote. Our life here is even
worse than in Gorokhovaya 2, and in a sense we are
being treated exactly like Russian officers and bourgeois, who are being slowly starved to death here.
Our only hope lies in parcels, but delivery of parcels
has been stopped for the moment. Those due on
Monday last have not yet been delivered. It all

depends on the caprice of some one in authority, and he seems very capricious. Surely we are entitled to be treated like prisoners of war and to be inspected by neutrals, to have the right of buying food, of getting news, of sending letters, of exercise, of getting clean linen, &c. Apart from the question of food, that of clothing and medical attention are most important. All the prisoners here have a chronic diarrhœa; most of us have now got it. Requests for a doctor, or medicine, or complaints to the commandant, all receive no attention. In short, our treatment is absolutely inhuman.

"Following is a short account of our treatment since Saturday last. We were never told why we were arrested, and from the first all requests, &c., to see you have been contemptuously and rudely refused. We reached Gorokhovaya at 6 P.M. on Saturday, and, after questioning of an aimless sort, we were put, at 8 P.M., in a room about 25 feet by 15 feet, where there were already about fifty arrested Russians—murderers, speculants [*sic*], &c. All beds were already occupied, and we spent the night between the three odd chairs, the floor, and walking about. By morning we were all in the first stages of verminosity, very dirty, tired, and hungry. The first food came at 1 P.M., small bowls of bad fish, soup, and one-eighth of a pound of bread. At 6 P.M. we got another one-eighth pound of bread. We received the same food on Monday also. On Sunday night the room was less full, and we got some sleep. By that time we were also getting used to the journey [*sic*]. Parcels arrived on Monday and eased the food situation. On Tuesday at 4 P.M. we were marched through the streets under escort here. The consul's request for a vehicle for our kit was most rudely refused. Here we were distributed in different cells, size about 20 feet by 10 feet, in order to make up the number twenty. In our cell are thirteen Russians, four of whom are slowly starving to death. They have had no food for three days. After we had been here thirty-three hours, soup came in at 3 A.M., and one-eighth pound of bread. We could not eat the soup; wood leather, stones, mixed with cabbage and paper, were its main ingredients. So we, too, will sooner or later starve to death. Our immediate need is parcels, but it is essential for you to send some one here on Saturday to see if they have been delivered and to obtain our receipts. Otherwise they will not be delivered.

"Next is medical comforts: (1) for diarrhœa; (2) aspirin. We can get none. Third is some money.

"We will write again to-morrow. We are not allowed to leave our cells. The door is never opened. The w.c. periodically refuses to work, and the atmosphere is appalling.

"Need I say more, save that I hope you will lay the substance of this report before His Majesty's Government.

"With many apologies for giving you this trouble.—(Signed) From British Subjects detained in Peter and Paul."

The fate of the Russian Imperial family

Mr. Alston to Mr. Balfour.—(Received September 18.)

(Telegraphic.)   *Vladivostock, September* 16, 1918.

HIS Majesty's consul at Ekaterinburg, Mr. Preston, who left that place on the 1st September, has just arrived here, and has given following information as to fate of Russian Imperial family:—

Ex-Emperor of Russia and Grand Duchess Tatiana were brought from Tobolsk to Ekaterinburg by Bolsheviks on the 1st May, 1918. Emperor was given suitable quarters near British consulate. Rest of Imperial family, including ex-Empress, other three daughters, and Czarevitch arrived a few days later. Members of suite, including Prince Dolgorouki, as well as British and French tutors who came with Imperial family from Tobolsk, were not allowed to remain with Emperor at Ekaterinburg, and returned to Tobolsk. Prince Dolgorouki was kept in prison, where he either eventually died or was killed.

Prince Dolgorouki frequently asked me, as doyen of Consular Corps, at least to try and obtain better conditions of living for Imperial family. It was impossible for me, however, to do anything, and when I interceded for the Princess, whom I said I was protecting as a Serbian ally, I was threatened with arrest. When the Czech advance on Cheliabinsk commenced, the Ekaterinburg Bolshevik Government, who already had considerable friction with Central Bolshevik Government on money matters, began to use threats against the Imperial family as a means of extorting funds from Central Government. When Bolsheviks knew they would have to evacuate Ekaterinburg owing to the approach of the Czechs, they asked the people's commissaries at Moscow what they should do with the Emperor. The reply they received was: "Do whatever you think fit." At a meeting of the Ural Soldiers' and Workmen's delegates held on 16th July, a decision was come to that the Emperor should be shot, and this decision was communicated to him, and sentence carried out by Lettish soldiers same night. However, no trace has ever been found of the body. The rest of members of Imperial family were taken away to an unknown destination immediately after this. It is said that they were burnt alive, as various articles of jewellery have been identified as belonging to them by their old servants, and their charred remains are said to have been found in a house burnt to the ground. It is still thought possible that the Bolsheviks took them north when they retreated to Verhotoury. The following grand dukes were in captivity near Ekaterinburg, at Alapaevsk, besides the ex-Emperor, George Constantinovitch, Ivan Constantinovitch, and Serge Michailovitch. Princess Helene of Serbia, the wife of the Grand Duke Ivan Constantinovitch, was frequently at the British consulate, where everything possible was done for her, but in spite of my energetic protests, the Bolsheviks took the Princess with them when they evacuated the town.

With the help of local White Guards, the three above-mentioned grand dukes managed to escape from their captivity, but it is not known where they are at present.

Sir C. Eliot to Mr. Balfour.—(Received January 2, 1919.)

Sir,   *Ekaterinburg, October* 5, 1918.
I HAVE the honour to submit the following report of what is known respecting the fate of the Russian Imperial family, as well as a short narrative written at my request by Mr. Sidney Gibbes, formerly tutor to His Imperial Highness the Czarevitch. Mr. Gibbes

accompanied the Imperial children from Tobolsk to Ekaterinburg on 23rd May, but was not allowed to live in the house where they were confined with their parents in the latter town.

The Bolsheviks of Ekaterinburg stated in speeches and proclamations that the Czar was shot on the night of 16th July, but many of the best-informed Russians believe that he is still alive and in German custody. I dare not, however, indulge the hope that this is true, unless some more adequate explanation than those current can be given of the supposed action of the Bolsheviks.

The official in charge of the enquiry at the time of my visit showed me over the house where the Imperial family resided. He dismissed as pure inventions the stories commonly believed in Siberia, such as that the corpse had been discovered, or that a member of the firing party had made a confession. On the other hand, he said that all the narratives of persons who thought they had seen the Emperor after 16th July had proved to be entirely without foundation. In his own opinion, the chances were four to three that the murder had been perpetrated. The house stands on the side of a hill, and the entrance leads into the first floor, where the Imperial family lived; the ground floor, in which the guard was quartered, consisting of offices and kitchens. The latter, however, were not used for cooking, the only food allowed being military rations brought in from outside, and some special dishes for the Czarevitch which were supplied by the nuns of a neighbouring convent. A high wooden palisade hid the windows of the upper storey, which were also whitewashed inside and kept closed even in the heat of summer.

The Imperial family had to endure considerable hardships and insolence while they lived in this house. They were allowed only one walk of fifteen minutes in the garden every day, but the Czar found distraction in doing carpentering work in an open shed. At meals the soldiers sometimes came in and took part of the meat off the table, saying that there was too much, and the Imperial family were not allowed decent privacy.

The rooms when I saw them presented a melancholy and dirty appearance, because the Bolsheviks had burnt a great quantity of objects in the stoves, and the ashes were subsequently taken out by the police and spread on the tables and floor with the object of discovering if they contained anything interesting.

There appears to be no evidence whatever to corroborate the popular story that on the night of the 16th July the Czar was taken out of the house and shot by a firing party in the manner usual at Bolshevik executions, but there is some evidence that sounds of uproar and shooting were heard in the house that night, and that no traffic was allowed in the streets near it. The murder is believed to have taken place in a room on the ground floor, which was sealed up, but kindly opened for my inspection. It was quite empty; the floor was of plain wood, and the walls of wood coated with plaster. Doggerel verses and indecent figures were scrawled on them. On the wall opposite the door, and on the floor, were the marks of seventeen bullets, or, to be more accurate, marks showing where pieces of the wall and floor had been cut out in order to remove the bullet holes, the officials charged with the investigation having thought fit to take them away for examination elsewhere. They stated that Browning revolver bullets were found in all the holes, and that some of them were stained with blood. Otherwise no traces of blood were visible, but there were some signs that the wall had been scraped and washed. The position of the bullets indicated that the victims had been shot when kneeling, and that other shots had been fired into them when they had fallen on the floor. Mr. Gibbes thought that for religious reasons the Czar and Dr. Botkine would be sure to kneel when facing death. There is no real evidence as to who or how many the victims were, but it is supposed that they were five, namely, the Czar, Dr. Botkine, the Empress's maid, and two lackeys. No corpses were discovered, nor any trace of their having been disposed of by burning or otherwise, but it was stated that a finger bearing a ring, believed to have belonged to Dr. Botkine, was found in a well.

On the 17th July a train with the blinds down left Ekaterinburg for an unknown destination, and it is believed that the surviving members of the Imperial family were in it.

It will be seen from the above account that the statement of the Bolsheviks is the only evidence for the death of the Czar, and it is an easy task for ingenious and sanguine minds to invent narratives giving a plausible account of His Imperial Majesty's escape. It must indeed be admitted that since the Empress and her children, who are believed to be still alive, have totally disappeared, there is nothing unreasonable in supposing the Czar to be in the same case. The marks in the room at Ekaterinburg prove at most that some persons unknown were shot there, and might even be explained as the result of a drunken brawl.

But I fear that another train of thought is nearer to the truth. It seems to me eminently probable that the Bolsheviks of Moscow, or a section of them, wished to hand over the Czar to the Germans. With this object a commissioner went to Tobolsk and removed Their Imperial Majesties in a summary, but not unkindly, manner, probably intending to take them to Moscow. He evidently knew that the temper of the Siberian Bolsheviks was doubtful, for he stopped the train outside Omsk and, finding that the local authorities intended to arrest the Czar, he ordered the train to leave for Ekaterinburg, that is, to take the only other route to Moscow. But when the train reached Ekaterinburg it was stopped by the local authorities and all the occupants removed. Subsequently the Imperial children were brought to Ekaterinburg from Tobolsk and placed in custody with their parents. The treatment of the Imperial family at Ekaterinburg shows an animus which was entirely wanting at Tobolsk, and the Bolsheviks became more hostile and more suspicious, as they felt that their own reign was coming to an end, and that they must leave the city.

There is some evidence that they were much alarmed by an aeroplane flying over the garden of the house, and I fear it is comprehensible that in a fit of rage and panic they made away with His Imperial Majesty.

It is the general opinion in Ekaterinburg that the Empress, her son, and four daughters were not murdered, but were dispatched on the 17th July to the north or west. The story that they were burnt in a house seems to be an exaggeration of the fact that in a wood outside the town was found a heap of ashes, apparently the result of burning a considerable quantity of clothing. At the bottom of the ashes was a diamond, and, as one of the Grand Duchesses is said to have sewn a diamond into the lining of her cloak, it is supposed that the clothes of the Imperial family were burnt here. Also hair, identified as belonging to one of the Grand Duchesses, was found in the house. It therefore seems probable that the Imperial family were disguised before their removal. At Ekaterinburg I did not hear even a rumour as to their fate, but subsequent stories about the murder of various Grand Dukes and Grand Duchesses cannot but inspire apprehension.

I have, &c.

C. ELIOT

Memorandum Written by Mr. Sydney Gibbes, formerly Tutor of the Czarevitch, and given to me (High Commissioner) on October 5, at Ekaterinburg.

THE Emperor had no great cause to complain of his treatment while living in Tobolsk, and physically he greatly improved in health. He seemed to feel that he had absolved himself of a wearisome business and thrown the responsibility on other shoulders. The enforced leisure gave him more time to devote to what was undoubtedly dearest to him in the world— his wife and family. The Empress suffered more, but bore bravely up under all hardship.

The Grand Duchesses were always happy and contented, and seemed satisfied with the simple life to which they were reduced, although they pined for more exercise in the open air, the yard being a poor substitute for the parks. This indeed seemed generally to be their greatest hardship.

The Grand Duke enjoyed fairly good health most of the time, and suffered most from lack of youthful society, although the doctor's son was sometimes allowed to enter and play with him.

This simple family life went on till the beginning of April, when the first important Bolshevik Commissar, Yakovlef, arrived from Moscow. He was received by the Emperor, who showed him the rooms in which they lived, including the Grand Duke's room, where he was then lying ill in bed. At the end of the visit he asked to be taken a second time to see the Grand Duke.

After lunch on the 12th of April, Yakovlef announced to the Emperor and Empress that he was instructed to remove the Emperor, and hoped that he would consent and not oblige him to use force. The Empress was greatly distressed, and at her desire was allowed to accompany the Emperor and take with her her third daughter, the Grand Duchess Marie. Hasty

preparations were made for their departure. The
Imperial family dined alone, but at eleven o'clock
invited all who were accustomed to dine with them
to tea in the drawing-room. Tea was served at a large
round table carried into the room, and was a very sad
meal. The departure was fixed for 3 A.M., and shortly
before that time carts and carriages entered the yard.
The Emperor drove with Yakovlef, and the Empress
and Grand Duchess Marie in a half-covered tarantass.
They were accompanied by Prince Dolgorouki, Dr.
Botkine, the Empress's maid (Demidova), the
Emperor's man (Chemidorof), and one lackey
(Saidnef). The carriages were strewn with hay, on
which they sat, or rather reclined. The roads were in
a fearful condition, the thaws having already begun,
and at one point they were obliged to cross the river
on foot, the ice being already unsafe. On the second
night, they spent a few hours in a hut, and arrived on
the following day at Tumen, where a train was in
waiting which took them in the direction of Omsk.
Some versts outside that town Yakovlef left the train
and went by motor car to the telegraph station to
communicate with Moscow, and, finding that preparations were being made in Omsk to arrest the
Imperial family, he returned to the train, which then
left in the opposite direction, and returned the way it
came. However, on arrival at Ekaterinburg, the train
was stopped and everybody removed: Prince
Dolgorouki to prison and the others to a private
house in the centre of the town that had hastily been
prepared for their reception. A high wooden fence of

rough boards was hastily put up outside the house, and the windows whitened within. Here the Emperor, Empress, and Grand Duchess Marie lived till the 16th July, the rest of the children being brought from Tobolsk to join their parents on the 23rd of May. For this journey elaborate arrangements were made for its safe conduct, and the whole personal effects of the Imperial family, as well as the furniture from the Governor's house, were removed at the same time. The train arrived in the middle of the night, but was kept moving in and out of the station all night, and at 7 A.M. the children were removed, being placed in cabs and taken to the house. The night was cold and heavy snow fell as they left. At tea the Countess Hendrichof, the Empress's Lady-in-Waiting, Mlle. Schneider, the Empress's reader in Russian, and General Tatischef were taken away to the prison and have since been shot. At 11, three lackeys, the cook, and his boy were ordered to prepare to go into the house, and two certainly, most probably four, were afterwards shot. The remainder of the establishment, consisting of the Baroness Buxhoevden, Lady-in-Waiting to the Empress, the English and French tutors, and about sixteen personal attendants and servants were set at liberty and happily escaped.

Since the departure of the Bolsheviks, the house in which the Imperial family lived has been thoroughly examined, and undoubted traces of murder exist, but the number of shots are not sufficient to warrant the supposition that all the persons there confined were murdered. Part were murdered and part were taken away, and as the Grand Duchesses' hair had been found, it is supposed that the Imperial children were taken away disguised. Garments having been burnt in a forest outside the town also strengthens this supposition. The Bolsheviks announced after this date at a public meeting held in the theatre and by bills posted on the walls that the Emperor had been shot and the Imperial family removed to a safe place, and to the present there is no evidence to prove the statement false, while the evidence of the hair would prove that at least the part of the statement concerning the children was true. But since that date nearly three months have passed.

Other members of the Imperial family confined at Alapaevsk, a small town 100 versts from Ekaterinburg, included the Grand Duke Serge Michaelovitch, Prince John Constantinovitch, Prince Igor Constantinovitch, and Count Vladimir Pavlovitch Palé, all of whom there is reason to fear have been killed. The Grand Duchess Serge, who was also there is reported to have been wounded and taken away. Princess Helen Petrovna, of Serbia, who came to Ekaterinburg to be near her husband, was arrested, as well as the two Serbian officers who came to induce her to leave, and has been removed with the other hostages taken from the town.

Mr. Alston to Mr. Balfour.—(Received November 5.)

(Telegraphic.)   *Vladivostock, November 4, 1918.*
FOLLOWING from Consul at Ekaterinburg, 28th October:—

"Regret to report I am informed by Russian staff that when Alapaevsk was taken by Russian troops on 29th September corpses, sufficiently preserved to be recognised, of Grand Duchess Elizabeth Feodorovna, and of three Royal Princes John, Constantin, and Igor Constantinovitch, and also that of Grand Duke Serge Michaelovitch, and lady-in-waiting, name yet unknown, were found in mine pit in which they had been thrown, presumably alive, bombs being thrown on them which did not effectually explode. All were buried with ceremonial, large crowds attending. Princess Helene of Serbia, believed to be at Perm, where she was taken by Bolsheviks with Serbian mission, when Bolsheviks evacuated Ekaterinburg. Making thorough investigation."

Mr. Lockhart to Sir G. Clerk.

Dear Sir George,   *November* 10, 1918.

THE following points may interest Mr. Balfour:—

1. The Bolsheviks have established a rule of force and oppression unequalled in the history of any autocracy.

2. Themselves the fiercest upholders of the right of free speech, they have suppressed, since coming into power, every newspaper which does not approve their policy. In this respect the Socialist press has suffered most of all. Even the papers of

the Internationalist Mensheviks like "Martov" have been suppressed and closed down, and the unfortunate editors thrown into prison or forced to flee for their lives.

3. The right of holding public meetings has been abolished. The vote has been taken away from everyone except the workmen in the factories and the poorer servants, and even amongst the workmen those who dare to vote against the Bolsheviks are marked down by the Bolshevik secret police as counter-revolutionaries, and are fortunate if their worst fate is to be thrown into prison, of which in Russia to-day it may truly be said, "many go in but few come out."

4. The worst crimes of the Bolsheviks have been against their Socialist opponents. Of the countless executions which the Bolsheviks have carried out a large percentage has fallen on the heads of Socialists who had waged a life-long struggle against the old régime, but who are now denounced as counter-revolutionaries merely because they disapprove of the manner in which the Bolsheviks have discredited socialism.

5. The Bolsheviks have abolished even the most primitive forms of justice. Thousands of men and women have been shot without even the mockery of a trial, and thousands more are left to rot in the prisons under conditions to find a parallel to which one must turn to the darkest annals of Indian or Chinese history.

6. The Bolsheviks have restored the barbarous

methods of torture. The examination of prisoners frequently takes place with a revolver at the unfortunate prisoner's head.

7. The Bolsheviks have established the odious practice of taking hostages. Still worse, they have struck at their political opponents through their women folk. When recently a long list of hostages was published in Petrograd, the Bolsheviks seized the wives of those men whom they could not find and threw them into prison until their husbands should give themselves up.

8. The Bolsheviks who destroyed the Russian army, and who have always been the avowed opponents of militarism, have forcibly mobilised officers who do not share their political views, but whose technical knowledge is indispensable, and by the threat of immediate execution have forced them to fight against their fellow-countrymen in a civil war of unparalleled horror.

9. The avowed ambition of Lenin is to create civil warfare throughout Europe. Every speech of Lenin's is a denunciation of constitutional methods, and a glorification of the doctrine of physical force. With that object in view he is destroying systematically both by executions and by deliberate starvation every form of opposition to Bolshevism. This system of "terror" is aimed chiefly at the Liberals and non-Bolshevik Socialists, whom Lenin regards as his most dangerous opponents.

10. In order to maintain their popularity with the

working men and with their hired mercenaries, the Bolsheviks are paying their supporters enormous wages by means of an unchecked paper issue; until to-day money in Russia has naturally lost all value. Even according to their own figures the Bolsheviks' expenditure exceeds the revenue by thousands of millions of roubles per annum.

These are facts for which the Bolsheviks may seek to find an excuse, but which they cannot deny.

Yours sincerely,

R. H. B. LOCKHART.

∘∘⊰⧳⧳⊱∘∘

REPORTS ON CONDITIONS IN RUSSIA

**Report on "Bolshevik Realities," by Mrs.
L—, formerly Organiser and Controller of a
large War Hospital in Moscow, who left Russia
in October 1918.**

The Peasants and the Land.—Already under the
régime of the Provisional Government the land had
been handed over to the whole body of the peasants
in each district. But it must be borne in mind that the
Russian peasant has a strongly developed sense of

property and all his hopes were centred on an ulti-
mate dividing of the land, which would make each
one an individual proprietor and guarantee him the
secure ownership of his holding. The Bolsheviks,
however, regarding the land as the property of the
nation as a whole, ordered the peasants to cultivate
the fields for the benefit of the local commune. The
peasants, disappointed in their hopes, soon began to
express their disapproval of the new policy. This
brought upon them the accusation of disloyalty to the
Soviet Government, and their antagonism was coun-
tered by the appointment in each district of
"Comiteti Bednoti" (Committees consisting of the
poorest class of peasants), who disposed of the crop,
leaving a certain amount in possession of those who
had grown it and taking the rest for themselves. This
meant that the drones got all they needed without
doing any productive work, and was equivalent to a
premium on idleness. The inevitable result was a
steady decline in the crops, which will in the end
prove the ruin of agricultural Russia.

The Factory and the Workmen.—Under the
Provisional Government, Workmen's Committees
were formed which dealt with such questions as hir-
ing of labour, deciding the scale of pensions,
allowances, and bonuses, and the whole administration of the factory. Selling prices were controlled and
profits were allocated in the proportion of 95 per
cent. to the State and 5 per cent. to the owner. In
practice this scheme resulted in continual reconstruc-

tion of the committees on the ground that the bonuses were too low or pensions unfairly awarded. The committees were never in power long enough to get acquainted with the details of the business. At the beginning of their régime the Bolsheviks did not alter this system, but gradually changes leading towards nationalisation were inaugurated. In March 1918 private trade was put an end to and a Central Board for every industry was set up which collected the produce from various firms. The selling prices were fixed by decree, but payment out of which wages and expenses had to come was made by the Central Board only after long delay and repeated demand.

In July all factories were nationalised and handed over to the workmen under the direction of Central Boards which functioned in a most despotic manner. All owners and managers were turned out and could not re-enter the works unless elected. At the slightest opposition or protest the workmen were thrown into prison, field guns brought out, and the threat made to raze the factory to the ground.

Wages and Food.—The minimum wage for a workman was fixed at 500 roubles per month, while superior artisans (a very small percentage of the community) received up to a maximum of 1,000 roubles per month. This sum was fixed on the assumption that the official rations were inadequate. In actual fact the scale was ludicrously insufficient to maintain life. Up till September 1916 the bread ration was 1/4 lb. to 1/2 lb. per day for workmen and 1/6 lb. for others. The bread was of very low standard, was full of refuse of all kinds and of the consistency of putty. Even this ration was seldom to be had. True, certain things could be obtained by underhand means, as for example black flour at 10 roubles per lb. (equivalent to 6 s. to-day), butter at 39 roubles per lb., sugar at 39 roubles per lb., eggs at 27 roubles per dozen. From this it is quite evident that the wage of 500 roubles was inadequate for the upkeep of a family. As a result the workpeople tried to bring supplies into the town from districts where the prices were lower. This practice was strongly forbidden by the Government because it upset their "rationing organisation," and strong measures were taken to repress it. A train returning from one of the food areas would be held up by a body of Red Guards, established at some point on the line. These guards would open fire on the train and almost invariably some of the passengers were shot. All had their provisions confiscated, and the wretched workman returned to his home minus money and flour and having lost two or three days' work. These food hunting expeditions disorganised the whole of the factories, as a third of the men were always absent. When it is remembered that clothing, rent, and other necessaries had also to be provided out of the 500 roubles, it will be understood how deplorable were the conditions of life. Materials and made-up clothing were also rationed, but there was hardly enough to supply the needs of one-tenth of the population. The result of this struggle between the workmen and the Government, and the inefficiency of the latter's subordinate officials, is that the Russian factories are rapidly falling into a state of ruin. Output has decreased in some cases 90 per cent., and as there is no available supply of fuel or raw materials it is only a question of a few months, if the Bolsheviks remain in power, before the factories will be forced to close down.

Repression of Democracy.—After the July Congress and the anti-Bolshevik demonstration of the Left Social Revolutionaries, non-Bolshevik Socialists were deprived of all political rights, hundreds of Socialist workmen were thrown into prison and large numbers were shot. In addition 3,000 workmen were thrown out of employment in the tramway repairing shops in Moscow simply on the ground of their Social Revolutionary sympathies.

The best illustration of the autocratic rule under which the workmen now exist is the fact that all public expression of opinion has been forbidden. All non-Bolshevik newspapers have been suppressed, including even "the Independent Socialist," whose editor, Martov, had a world-wide reputation in Socialist circles. All public meetings except those organised by the Bolsheviks are prohibited, and the Bolsheviks call themselves "the Peasants' and Workmen's Government."

The most serious crime in the eyes of the Bolsheviks is anti-Bolshevism, and the work of discovering and punishing offenders of this kind is in the hands of the Extraordinary Commission—an autocratic body which arrests, examines, imprisons, and executes at will. There is no charge, no public trial, and no appeal. There are English works-foremen in prison in Moscow to-day with nothing against them except the fact that they happened to be in a certain street or square at the time when the Red Guards took it into their heads to make a general arrest. Appeals from the Red Cross and the neutral consuls are unavailing. The Kommissar in charge of the case is away ill and nothing can be done till his return. Crimes of street robbery, &c., are punished in a rough-and-ready way; the offender is shot on the spot and the body left there till some one thinks good to remove it.

To describe the life inside the prisons would require the pen of Charles Reade.* Even using the greatest restraint and moderation, any account must appear exaggerated and hysterical to English readers. In verminous, ill-ventilated cells, starved and ter-rorised people are crowded together in one room, men, women, young girls (the latter held as hostages to force their hiding fathers or brothers to give them-selves up). At six o'clock in the evening the doors are locked and no one is allowed out for any reason till morning, except those called out at about 3 A.M. for execution. Healthy and sick (some with cholera) are huddled on the floor, uncertain of their fate and knowing it is out of the power of anyone to help them. The food consists of one quarter of a pound of black bread and a bowl of hot water in which are

* Charles Reade (1814–1884): novelist and playwright, the author of *The Cloister and the Hearth*.

floating some pieces of cabbage and occasionally a few fish heads. Red Cross officials noticed a rapid change in the appearance of prisoners; they looked each day more haggard, drawn, and hopeless.

Report by Mr. H—, Vladimir.—October 14, 1918.

OUR mills continued to work under the most adverse conditions, which grew from bad to worse during the course of the years 1917–1918, owing to labour disorganisation, shortage of raw material, money (from a balance of 35,000,000 roubles we now owe 25,000,000 roubles to the State Bank), and finally of food for the workpeople. The large shell manufacturing plant which during the course of the war we had developed had to be closed down by orders of the Soviet. Famine and cholera finally made their appearance, and the workpeople and their families (especially children) commenced to die and to grow so weak as to seriously impair their capacity for work. My co-directors and self were powerless to do anything to help or do anything in the matter as the Soviet had taken over everything connected with the working of the concern, putting in utterly incapable people such as doorkeepers, watchmen, &c., to supervise work demanding long experience, technical and medical knowledge, even interfering with the hospital administration, where the man cook supervised the work of our doctors.

As the mill position grew worse and matters became impossible I was charged with sabotage and working as an agent of England to paralyse industry in our district. All the sales and purchases of materials and goods were made through the agency of the Soviet, who employed dishonest persons with the result that though our goods were ostensibly sold to various representative bodies such as other Soviet organisations, in reality they were made the objects of speculation and theft, and sold in some cases to known German agents and sent to Germany. This was known to the workpeople who were greatly excited by the matter. Shortage of food, the supply and disposal of which became a Soviet monopoly, with the usual result of stopping all supplies, forced the workpeople to travel to the grain districts in the South and East of Russia and obtain supplies there themselves.

The supplies, in order to preserve the principle of Soviet monopoly, were usually confiscated by the Red Army requisition commandoes from the unfortunate people on their return journeys on the railways. These Red Army requisition commandoes are charged with the duty of stopping all private trading and so-called speculation, but being in many cases utterly devoid of any idea of honesty or duty, merely took the food and resold same, in many cases to the people again. Eventually there was no more money to be had, the workpeople having even exhausted their savings. In addition, the journey undertaken to obtain food was long, costly and arduous, and generally 50 per cent. of the people were away from their occupation, losing their wages and so making their position still worse, and congesting the railways.

At the same time members of the local Soviet were continually seen in a drunken condition and were evidently living well. Exasperation grew, and finally the workpeople, with whom joined many of the peasants in the district, came in a body to me and asked my aid, but I was powerless to help. In addition, I had to be very careful as my words and actions could have been so misconstrued to the Soviet as to cause them to think that I was interfering in their functions. The fact of the people coming to me as of old for help alarmed the Soviet authorities, and open threats were made against me and arrests of workmen followed. This was at the time of the outrage at the British Embassy at Petrograd, and on receipt of news of same I was advised to leave by certain members of the Soviet.

A meeting was then called by order of the Moscow authorities in order to choose the quota of members of the requisition commandoes of the Red Army from amongst the workpeople, who answered the summons by picking the members of the local Soviet, who were bitterly attacked and the actions and authority of the Soviet Government repudiated. The speakers were arrested, and on the demand of the crowd of workpeople, numbering some 20,000, to release them, the guard of the local prison consisting of members of the Red Army opened fire, killing and wounding, it was stated, over 100 people. In addition many were badly hurt in the panic which ensued. On the following day all the mills and works in the district were stopped, the workpeople striking as a protest.

I then left the district for Moscow, not wishing to

be made the centre of an anti–Soviet movement: especially as the authorities were accusing the British and French representatives as being the cause of the many disturbances which were occurring all over the country, but which in reality were caused by their own reckless, unscrupulous, and utterly dishonest conduct.

My house, with all contents, horses, carriages, clothing, &c., were confiscated or "requisitioned" by the local Soviet. In addition all my holding in the firm, including shares and loan money, were taken over by the Central Government, and jewellery, plate and papers placed in the safe of the library at the Anglican Church, and furs stored in cold storage in Moscow were confiscated by the Moscow Tribunal.

Recent legislation

ALL lands, buildings, machinery, &c., were now nationalised, without any compensation being paid to the former owners. The result has been an utter deadlock, all private enterprise being killed. Money is being hidden to an enormous extent, the absence of which is being made good as quickly as ever possible by the Soviet's printing presses; private printing establishments being taken over for this purpose. It is estimated that the quantity of paper currency in circulation is now over 30,000,000,000 roubles, roughly 100 times the present gold reserve.

A great quantity of false money is also being printed and being brought into circulation, especially the 20 and 40 rouble note varieties. All private trading is being taken over by the Government and the stocks are being confiscated.

Gold articles over a certain weight are confiscated, with the result that same have disappeared, being hidden by the owners. The system of education has been entirely altered. All religious instruction has been abolished, and in its place a form of State Socialistic instruction substituted. The peasantry now refuse to send their children to the State schools and they remain without education. Clothing, such as winter overcoats, belonging to private people are being confiscated for the benefit of the Red Army. No man is supposed to possess more than one suit of clothes, two changes of linen, or two pairs of boots; anything above this is requisitioned for so-called State purposes. All furniture is nationalised.

Political conditions

Throughout the districts occupied or administered by the Soviet Government 90 per cent. of the population is against the administration, and probably not more than 5 per cent. actively support the same. This 5 per cent. consists of returned political refugees, mostly non-Russian in race, members of the many committees, commissariats, and Government's Departments, Red Army recruits, who are receiving high wages, and a certain number of fanatics, mostly young, of both sexes. The remaining 5 per cent. support the Soviets simply owing to the fact that they are dependent on them for a living. Also amongst these there are a certain number who are working for the purpose of getting acquainted with the organisations. This element could be depended upon to give valuable help in the event of a counter-revolution. Feeling is very bitter amongst all classes of the working population and peasantry, but these people are now so terrified, and, in the case of the town-bred working population, so weakened physically, as to preclude any possibility of a rising against the ruling power for the present. Regarding the form of Government which the people desired, the majority, especially amongst the peasantry, wish a monarchy. From carefully-noted inquiries of peasants and workpeople I found that 90 per cent. were of this opinion.

Report by Mr. G.——, who left Petrograd in November, 1918.

WHEN we turn from the general aims of the Bolshevik policy to the actual situation in the big cities, as Petrograd and Moscow at the time when I left, it could be summed up in one word—famine. As regards Petrograd, its population now has come down to 908,000, whereas in 1916 it was estimated at 2,500,000 to 2,600,000 people. Two-thirds of the population have been able to escape to other parts of the country, and the one-third remaining is reduced to starvation. The prices for food have risen to such an extent that all the principal commodities are out of the reach of the buyer. The amount of food which is allowed by rations is in itself absolutely insufficient to keep up life, and then it is hardly regularly received; sometimes bread is not received for two days consecutively. Besides, it must not be forgotten that the Russian population is divided into four classes, the educated and capitalist class being put into the third and fourth category, receiving three or four times less than the workmen and other classes, who are in the first and respectable category. Even the workman who gets four times more than others cannot live on his ration, and must buy bread and other commodities in an underhand way, the open sale of them being forbidden.

In order to give an instance, I wish just to say that an egg cost, when I left, six roubles; a bottle of milk, six or seven roubles; a pound of bread, fourteen to seventeen roubles. The class which is the best fed is the Red Army and the Bolshevik officers.

The foreign press has, as I understand, published some details about the September massacres in Petrograd, when more than one thousand men were shot in Kronstadt and at the Peter-Paul Fortress indiscriminately, without any trial, not even the pretence of a court-martial; shot, or drowned, as was the case with Father Ornatsky, the well-known priest of the Kazan Cathedral in Petrograd, who was drowned with his two young sons, who were officers, along with many others. Whereas the shooting in big towns has during the last months decreased owing to Lenin's personal dislike of Red terrorism, it is continuing in the provinces, where priests, landowners, physicians, rich merchants, lawyers, are indiscriminately shot in cold blood, without any trial and without any reason besides a general pretext of being counter-revolutionists. Arrests and domestic searches are going on as before. There are some thousands of men and women starving in the prisons of Petrograd—professors of universities, eminent lawyers, priests, generals, officers, ladies of society, bankers, &c. There are towns and districts where all the priests who have to wear their hair long in accordance with religious custom now have been forced to have it cut short. In other towns churches have been desecrated and bishops arrested or shot.

A special measure, in order to complete the humiliation of the bourgeoisie, is compulsorily forced labour, to which all the bourgeoisie men and women are liable, and which consists in men from 20 to 60 being sent on all sorts of jobs, discharging of coal, cleaning water-closets in the soldiers' barracks, digging graves in cemeteries, removing cholera stricken patients, &c.; and for the women being obliged to wash the dirty linen of the barracks, or other like jobs for a month. In case of the women with delicate health, and of elderly men, death from exposure or severe illness after a week or two of such labour, which is usually conducted under the most humiliating conditions, is not seldom.

Under the conditions which I have outlined above it is not astonishing that disaffection is growing, and it must be said that it is growing in all classes of the population. It is evident that the attitude of the educated classes against Bolshevism is one of impotent hatred. The news given out by Bolshevik employees that the intellectual and bourgeoisie classes have allied themselves with the Bolsheviks is a deliberate falsehood. It is true that thousands upon thousands of these people have been induced to work under the Bolsheviks to accept some salaried situation with the government, but in respect to the working classes it must be borne in mind that the industrial working man has practically disappeared. Bolshevism has ruined Russian industry. The great bulk of the big factories, workshops, or mills do not work for a great many months, for want of raw materials. The workmen received from the State full pay for some time, but afterwards had to choose either to return to the villages or to enlist in the Red Army, and in most cases they did the latter. The small artisan is starving to death, which explains his anti-Bolshevik attitude. There remains the peasant, far away in his village, rich with paper money and bread, which he does not want to give away, but the Bolsheviks are sending armed expeditions to steal bread, which they want to feed the Red Army. The shooting of peasants every day by the Red Guards coming down for bread is an everyday feature. Revolutions have broken out, and nearly everywhere they are being quelled with blood.

When we ask ourselves who are the classes who support the Bolsheviks, the answer would be that they consist of the people who are fed and paid by the Bolsheviks, the Red Army, and the not less numerous army of paid Government officials. All of them are paid more and fed better than the population amongst whom they live, and, with the present food conditions, it is not astonishing that they stick to the Bolsheviks. The Red Army and the numerous army of different commissioners have also an unlimited opportunity of plundering the peaceful population, of which they avail themselves to an extent which, in the small provincial towns in the country, is simply terrifying, and which brings around the Bolsheviks all the lowest classes of the population. On the other hand, it must not be forgotten that Bolshevism had for many years its best recruits from among the young workmen of big factories, who, as stated above, have now enlisted in the Red Army, and who form the Socialist nucleus of the State.

All political parties are declared to be outside the pale of the law, as counter-revolutionary, and the old Socialist parties, if they try to make public opposition to the Bolshevist tyranny, fare no better than the Liberal parties. Especially the Socialist-Revolutionary party is subject to the most violent and bloody perse-cution. Under these circumstances, can it astonish anyone that public opinion, terrorised by imprison-ment and numberless executions, remains dumb?

It must not be forgotten that the Bolsheviks have formed small committees of the so-called poorest peasants in each village, who are armed with rifles, and often machine guns, and who, being representa-tive of the proletariat, have to exercise the dictatorship of the people over the village bour-geoisie, making up the majority of peasants. The well-to-do peasant is thus completely excluded from any public activity, and is kept terrorised by these committees, which in many cases are composed of the worst elements of the village, drunkards, ex-convicts, &c. Further, it cannot be doubted that the Russian people are worn out by the war and by the revolution, and that the love of peace which was always a permanent feature of its national character has been enhanced and has developed itself into an attitude of dumb suffering.

The impartial reader of the Bolshevist press, and it must be taken into consideration that there does not exist any press with the exception of the official one now in Russia, can read in these official papers every day articles and information about local revolts which happen daily in various parts of the country, mostly villages where the peasants rise in an entirely unorganised way against the power of the Soviet. In the second part of November such revolts have taken place in nearly all the districts of the Government of Moscow, and were suppressed mercilessly by the Red Army, composed to a considerable extent of Chinese and Letts.

As regards food distribution, it is admitted even by the Bolsheviks that in no department of Government is there so much corruption as among the numberless officials who control the food admin-istration. The organisation of the food distribution is, of course, mainly governed by the fact that there is scarcely any food to be distributed.

Russian industry is dead for the moment, and the Russian industrial workman has ceased to exist as a class for the time being. It is an extremely curious feature of the Russian Revolution that a movement which has proclaimed itself as social and democratic has achieved in the first instance total destruction of those social groups on which a social democratic organisation is mainly based, the class of the industrial workmen. All factories, all the important ones with a few exceptions of those who are still engaged on munition work, are stopped, and the industrial workman had either to return to the village with which he had no more ties in common or to enlist in the Red Army.

The younger generation of the workmen, men of 19 to 26 years, have to a great extent chosen the second alternative, and it is they who form the Bolshevik nucleus of the Red Army. To speak of the growing success of the management of industrial concerns by Soviet is an absolute misrepresentation. It would be sufficient in order to disprove this statement to cite the instance of the most important factories and works in Petrograd, Moscow and Nishny, where factories which engaged usually many thousands occupy now a few hundred men.

As regards Petrograd, the number of executions is usually taken at 1,300, though the Bolsheviks admitted only 500, but then they do not take into account many hundreds of officers, former civil servants and private individuals who were shot in Kronstadt, and in the Peter and Paul Fortress in Petrograd, without any special order from the Central authorities, by the discretion of the local Soviet; 400 were shot during one night in Kronstadt alone; three big graves were dug in the courtyard and the 400 placed before it, then they were shot one after another.

The Extraordinary Commission of Petrograd had on the orders of the day of one of their sittings the question of the application of torture. It is common knowledge that the unfortunate Jewish student who killed Britozsky was tortured three or four times before his execution.

The Oboukhoff works were, in their majority, supporters of the Social Revolutionary party, or of other moderate socialist organisations. They summoned a meeting of the workmen at which, by an overwhelming majority, a resolution was carried insisting upon the Bolsheviks putting an end to the civil war, and reconstructing the Government on lines which would admit the participation of all socialistic parties. The Bolsheviks answered with a general lock-out of the workmen and the closing of the Oboukhoff works.

The population is everywhere divided into four classes for purposes of rationing, the middle and "parasitic" classes, being in the third and fourth divisions, getting one-quarter or one-eighth of the rations accorded to the workmen and the clerks, but even these rations remain mostly on paper, as there is not food enough to give them.

Report by Colonel Kimens, Acting British Vice-Consul at Petrograd, dated November 12.

THERE have been no arrests of British subjects during the last few weeks, but they are exposed to continual humiliations, ill-treatments, and hardships, and are suffering great financial losses. Practically no difference is being made now between Russians and foreigners; they have to do forced labour; the flats are requisitioned, and occupants obliged to leave them at a few days' notice; the furniture may not be removed, as it has been declared national property, and clothes and provisions, above a small minimum, are confiscated.

The state of affairs in Russia is becoming daily more critical, and the reign of terror is assuming proportions which seem quite impossible, and are incompatible with all ideas of humanity and civilisation. Government, properly speaking, has ceased to exist in Russia, and the only work done by the Soviet authorities is inciting of class hatred, requisitioning and confiscation of property, and destruction of absolutely everything, and world propaganda of Bolshevism. All freedom of word and action has been suppressed; the country is being ruled by an autocracy which is infinitely worse than that of the old régime; justice does not exist, and every act on the part of persons not belonging to the "proletariat" is interpreted as counter-revolutionary and punished by imprisonment, and in many cases execution, without giving the unfortunate victim a chance of defending himself in a tribunal, as sentences are passed without trial.

The whole legislation of the country is done by decrees, which are published by the central Soviet authorities at Moscow and the northern commune at

Petrograd, and are supposed to be enforced everywhere, but in reality this remains only on paper and the local authorities obey only such orders from which they can derive a personal profit, and ignore all others. The chaos has gone so far that the central authorities are no longer obeyed, and as a result of it every province has become a state in a state. Anarchy is rampant everywhere, villages rise against villages, peasants against peasants, and the country is entering upon an era of open interior warfare, so that if this state of things is allowed to continue only the fittest will survive.

The *prima facie* reason of this state of affairs is the expropriation of landed property, and the subsequent abolition of all other property. This is the root of the whole evil which has brought Russia to the present condition.

The first step taken in this direction was the expropriation of landed property belonging to the peasants, followed by the nationalisation of town property and houses. In December 1917 the banks were seized, and soon afterwards began the nationalisation of works and factories. Now all furniture is being confiscated, and people are allowed to have only a small quantity of clothes. The nationalisation of trade which has now been decreed will be the final death-blow to life and Russia's productive power will come to an end.

This policy of the Soviet authorities can be easily explained, and is quite logical from their point of view. Their one object is to overthrow the existing order of things and capitalism, first in Russia and afterwards in all other countries, and in order to attain this end all methods are admissible as long as the masses remain satisfied. The expropriation of land has led to a very considerable decrease of crops, the nationalisation of factories to a standstill of industry, the seizure of the banks to a complete cessation of money circulation, and the nationalisation of trade to a deadlock in that branch of the economic life of the country, so that nothing is being produced, and there the system of the present policy of confiscation will be applied on an increasing scale, as the dissatisfaction of the masses cannot be admitted and the popularity of the authorities must be kept up.

It is obvious that the present rulers of Russia realise that this state of things cannot continue indefinitely, and that it is impossible to rule a country on confiscation and on a steadily increasing issue of paper money, which amounts at present to 3 milliards of roubles. The intention of the Government is to rule on these lines as long as possible, and afterwards to carry it on in other neighbouring countries, and as there are strong Bolshevik tendencies in Poland, the Ukraine, the Baltic Provinces, and in Finland, the danger is very great indeed that Bolshevism will spread in those countries. In that case it will be impossible to stop the movement which presents a danger to the civilisation of the whole world.

∽◦◦◦∽

Mr. Lindley to Mr. Balfour.—(Received November 28.)

(Telegraphic.) *Archangel, November* 27, 1918.

I VENTURE to lay the following considerations before you:—

There is nothing new in Bolshevik ideas of society. They were expressed in the sixties of last century by a certain Bakunin, commonly considered an anarchist. An exact description of them may be found on page 319 of volume II, 1905 edition, of Sir W. Wallace's work entitled "Russia." The book Lenin has written on the subject can add nothing essential to that description. It seems clear that no Government as at present constituted can safely have dealings with body of persons whose object is to overturn interests of Governments, especially those whose broad democratic base makes them most solid, and who have shown that no agreements they make will be allowed to stand in their way. Recent imprisonment of Persian Minister at Moscow because certain brigands from Turkestan have very properly been incarcerated by Persian Government, is an instance of the kind of difficulty any Government having dealings with Bolsheviks must be prepared to face at any moment.

Principal reason why Bolsheviks have lasted so long is their unlimited supply of paper money, and I venture to recommend particular attention be paid to this side of the problem. This paper money enables them not only to pay their way in Russia but to build up credits abroad, which are to be used to produce chaos in every civilised country. It is the first time in history that an anarchist society has unlimited resources.

I am absolutely convinced nothing is to be gained by having dealings with Bolsheviks. Over and over again they have shown themselves devoid of all scruples, and if it is inconvenient to punish their crimes and rid the world of them by force, the only alternative consistent with self-respect is to treat them like pariahs.

Sir C. Eliot to Mr. Balfour.—(Received November 30.)

(Telegraphic.) *Vladivostock, November* 29, 1918.

TELEGRAMS from vice-consul at Ekaterinburg state that officials are now coming to the conclusion that the Empress and her children were murdered in or near Ekaterinburg at the same time as the Emperor. Rest of evidence does not seem strong but dates may be significant. Emperor was murdered on the night of 16th July, and Grand Duke Serge, together with Princes mentioned in my telegram of 4th November, were murdered at Alapaevsk on 18th July. It is hence supposed that murderers went from Ekaterinburg to Alapaevsk. At Alapaevsk their intention was clearly to exterminate Imperial family, and it is feared they were actuated by same motive as at Ekaterinburg. At Tobolsk the victims were driven some distance out of the town and thrown into a pit. It is supposed that something of the same kind was done at Ekaterinburg, and it is possible that Empress and her children were taken a few miles by rail, which would account for idea that they were removed elsewhere.

Lord Kilmarnock to Mr. Balfour.—(Received December 6.)

Sir, *Copenhagen, November* 27, 1918.

I HAVE the honour to report that Mr. D—, director of a Petrograd Manufacturing Company, who has under his charge about 4,000 Russian workmen, and who is well acquainted with their views, called at His Majesty's Legation and stated that the position in Petrograd was as follows:—

In his opinion some 90 per cent. of the soldiers of the Red Guard are disaffected, and would desert the moment a well-organised force appeared if it were properly provided with supplies of food. The Guard consists largely of men who have become soldiers in order to escape starvation, and there is no revolutionary enthusiasm among them.

When he left Petrograd on the 16th instant the situation as regards food had improved slightly, but deaths from starvation were still a constant occurrence, especially among the intellectuals and those placed in unfavoured categories. The improvement was due to larger supplies of potatoes and vegetables arriving from the country. Flour, however, was still very scarce, only the soldiers and workmen could get bread. Horses were being slain, partly in order to provide food, partly because there was no fodder with which to feed them.

The transport difficulties in Petrograd were getting worse, and it was almost impossible to move the small quantities of rye and potatoes which reached the stations of the capital. The charge for a cab, which used to be 60 kopecks, was now 100 roubles, and Mr. D— who used to pay 10 roubles for the transport of a load of wood to his factory had now to pay 300 roubles. There was hardly any benzine for automobiles. The city was still lighted, but the scarcity of fuel was very acute.

Mr. D—'s factory had not been nationalised, and

owing to the stocks of raw materials which had been accumulated, the workmen, about 4,000, were still able to turn out about 7,000 pairs of shoes a day. Very few other factories, however, were working owing to the lack of raw material.

The power of the Bolsheviks has greatly diminished during the last six months, and the peasants in the villages round Petrograd were hostile to them, largely because their supplies were being commandeered by the soldiers. Though a small force would be sufficient to overthrow the Bolshevik rule, it would take a long time to establish order in the country, as the authorities had either disappeared or been killed, and the people had lost the habit of obedience.

Men were being shot every day, and the political terrorism continued.

The Red Guard had sent a notice to the Council of Workmen in Mr. D——'s factory, which had been shown to him in confidence by a faithful workman. It was worded as follows:—

"If there is anybody in the administration of the factory who is undesirable, please inform us."

And shortly afterwards two of his secretaries were arrested and imprisoned. Later they were released, but one at any rate will not recover from the hardships he endured in prison.

Three brothers named Stolyrow, who had a factory in the neighbourhood, had been denounced because they had been rough with their workmen, and had been shot.

Zinoviev (Apfelbaum) was still supreme in

Petrograd, and he still exercised a brutal reign of terror.

Mr. D— thought that the Bolsheviks were not contemplating an attack on Finland, as they were afraid of the Finnish army, but an attack on the Baltic provinces was likely, as the Bolsheviks desired to obtain food supplies and hoped to find supplies of potatoes, corn, &c., in Esthonia and Lettland.

I have, &c.
KILMARNOCK.

Memorandum on conditions in Moscow by a British subject, who left Moscow on December 1.

THE economic and social conditions in Moscow are in a state of chaos.

All trade and commerce—except illicit trading which is still carried on by the Jews—is at a complete standstill. The shops, even the smallest, are either closed or on the point of being closed, and all the places of business also.

On account of the fuel scarcity the compression

of the people in such houses as can be heated was becoming greater and greater. I was reduced from five rooms to one room, and was threatened with a further reduction.

Nothing was supposed to be obtainable except on the card system, and very little on that; clothing, boots, &c., were practically unobtainable, and even galoshes, so necessary in Russia, could hardly be got. Food without cards was still procurable at fabulous prices, but was every day getting scarcer. Milk was 5 roubles per glass; sugar, 50 roubles per pound; butter, 80 roubles per pound; tea, 125 roubles per pound; coffee, 100 roubles per pound; black flour, 10 roubles per pound.

This is not because there is a serious dearth of these foodstuffs—on the contrary, there is plenty of everything (except perhaps coffee) in the country, but because the Bolsheviks will not allow it to be brought into Moscow. They have divided the people into four categories—and only the two lowest, consisting of workpeople and employees of the Soviet, can get enough to live on, the other two are meant to starve. The different centrals, like the sugar central, the tea central, and the textile central, were in a state of helpless, hopeless chaos. Full of employees who had little or nothing to do—only half heated, and with huge queues of waiting people who cannot get the information, &c., they want.

The stability of the Soviet did not appear to me to be very great. It depended entirely on the well-paid Lettish battalions. Certainly the mass of the workpeople and peasants was not behind it. Many of the people working for it were only doing so to preserve themselves from starvation.

It was estimated that the Red Army consisted of about 200,000 fighting men. Many more were being drilled—but so little dependence was placed on them that they were not entrusted with arms. Meetings of workmen to discuss the mobilisation order openly decided to comply with it, because it was the easiest way of procuring food and clothing, but to decline to fight.

Great difficulty was encountered in getting regiments to leave Moscow for the front, and on many occasions trains intended to convey such troops were delayed for days. It was only by means of heavy disbursements that men were eventually induced to leave. It was reported that Moscow was almost denuded of troops and artillery. I was told that there were no guns for the Pskoff front, all having been sent south.

There is no actual food famine in Russia; on the contrary, there are enormous stocks of foodstuffs which could be spared for the rest of Europe. There is a famine, however, in articles of clothing and agricultural implements. Outside of Moscow and Petrograd, and, perhaps, some other centres, food was procurable at comparatively moderate prices, and in exchange for textile products even at really low prices. It is the disorganisation in the transport service, and the shortness of goods which the peasants need, coupled with the decrees of the Bolsheviks, which have brought about the present shortage of foodstuffs in certain localities.

I don't know what is the signification of the terms "Red" and "Cold" terrors.

All I can say is that the number of people who have been coldly done to death in Moscow is enormous. Many thousands have been shot, but lately those condemned to death were hung instead, and that in the most brutal manner. They were taken out in batches in the early hours of the morning to a place on the outskirts of the town, stripped to their shirts, and then hung one by one by being drawn up at the end of a rope until their feet were a few inches from the ground and then left to die. The work was done by Mongolian soldiers. Shooting was too noisy and not sure enough. Men have crawled away after a volley, and others have been buried while still alive. I was told in Stockholm by one of the representatives of the Esthonian Government that 150 Russian officers who were taken prisoners at Pskoff by the Red Guards were given over to the Mongolian soldiers, who sawed them in pieces.

◦◦✕◦◦

Mr. Alston to Mr. Balfour.—(Received January 4.)

(Telegraphic.) *Vladivostock, January* 2, 1919.

I HAVE derived following information, which may be considered authentic, with regard to position in Moscow, partly from the Vladivostock press, and partly from persons having connections there:—

With the exception of the Bolsheviks, the whole population is terrorised almost to a point of physical paralysis and imbecility. Slender supplies of even the simplest food are only to be had when the watch of the Bolshevik guard weakens, and three-quarters of the people are slowly starving to death. At the expense of the poor, hoarders see their chance to realise enormous profits. Throughout the daylight hours, long queues wait to try to get half-pound of tea, potatoes, or a bit of fish. Tea may be anything up to 100 roubles per pound, coarse black bread varies from 15 to 20 roubles per pound, according to the section of the town in which it is sold, and sugar is 50 roubles a pound, when obtainable. A second-hand suit of clothes costs anything up to 2,000 roubles, and a pair of boots 800 roubles. Horseflesh is the mainstay of the population at present, but even supplies of that are fast dwindling. Five hundred hostages were taken to Kronstadt for reprisals, soon after attempted assassination of Lenin, and these were subjected to most horrible tortures. The people often prefer to starve rather than risk torture at the hands of Chinese and Lettish hooligans who form "militia" on streets, and cower in their cellars, numbed with cold. To avoid extermination, the "intellectuals" have largely gone into the service of Bolsheviks. Their wages are insignificant if compared even with the camp followers of Bolshevik garrisons, who, at any rate, get fed fairly regularly.

All officers were ordered in July to report to Alexandrovsky school to be registered. About 20,000 appeared, and were shut up for three days without air, food, or sleep. Many went mad, and Lettish and Chinese guard mercilessly bayonetted those who attempted to escape when they were finally let out.

Residents in area round Butirsky prison abandoned their houses owing to the numerous
executions of "counter-revolutionary intellectuals."

Every day typhoid and tuberculosis are increasing, and ordinary population are quite unable to
procure medical supplies even at the most outrageous
prices.

Infants have been nationalised and become property of State upon attaining the age of eighteen.

As Petrograd has ceased to be the Bolshevik
headquarters, military situation there is better. In spite
of this, after the murder of Uritsky, the Bolshevik
commissary, the town virtually ran with blood.
Owing to there being less food even than in Moscow,
the death toll from disease is much higher. This is also
due to the fact that, without being buried, corpses of
horses, dogs, and human beings lie about in the
streets.

Cholera took very heavy toll in summer, as all the
canals are polluted with decomposed bodies of men
and animals.

Things are considerably better on Viborg side, but
although Bolsheviks get food themselves, they take
good care that none gets to the bourgeoisie from
Finland side.

It may be considered that whole population of
Petrograd is virtually insane, if not hunger-stricken,
and, unlike the people in Moscow, who have suffered
less, it is unable to appreciate possibility of utter extermination of educated elements. To release and provide
food for themselves and their armies, Bolsheviks will

be forced ultimately to kill off the greater portion of population. In any of big towns, as at Petrograd, Moscow, and Kursk, a horrible massacre is possible at any moment.

Mr. Alston to Mr. Balfour.—(Received January 4.)

(Telegraphic.)   *Vladivostock, January* 3, 1919.
ALTHOUGH I am sure it has not escaped your notice, I venture to draw your attention to a feature in situation, when considering future policy in Russia.

There will be serious shortage of foodstuffs in Europe so long as the fields of Russia are unproductive, or their produce is unable to be exported, as Russia is the principal granary of Europe and supplies all the contiguous States with the bulk of their imported cereals.

During present winter it is practically certain that, owing to disorganisation brought about by efforts of Lenin and Trotsky, tens, if not hundreds of thousands of Russians will perish from starvation. The 1919 harvests will amount only to a fraction of pre-war productions if there is no marked improvement of internal situation before early spring. The Allies and other nations will find themselves morally bound to export foodstuffs to Russia to avert a catastrophe during present winter, instead of importing foodstuffs from Russia during winter of 1919-1920. Certain parties in Allied countries represent military intervention as forcible repression of working classes at instigation of capitalists, and not merely as an effort to restore order and render Russia once more self-supporting. Of course this is what Bolsheviks maintain, and they justify their excesses and atrocities on the pretext that they are engaged in a struggle against capitalism abroad and at home. Their deluded followers support them, not because they believe this, but because Bolsheviks control food supplies, and alternative to joining them is starvation. The fact that alternative is starvation will soon be plain to neutral countries. For a few months population may subsist on plunder and devastation, but the result is inevitable when all creative and productive enterprise is at a standstill.

Currency has been wrecked, all industries have been destroyed, and labour has been encouraged to believe that instead of working to obtain livelihood, there are easier methods of obtaining it. The whole country will be suffering from disorganisation of currency and transport, unless more energetic measures are adopted for restoration of order, and it will be impossible to produce harvests adequate for population.

Intervention on a larger scale than hitherto attempted would therefore seem necessary if the situation is to be saved before the next harvests are sown.

It is absurd to pretend that effective military intervention would be an espousal of cause of capitalism against labour and an act of oppression. Destruction and production are the forces opposed, not capitalism and labour. It seems to be the duty of the Allies, not only to themselves, but to humanity, to restore order in Russia.

Mr. Alston to Mr. Balfour.—(Received January 6.)

(Telegraphic.)   *Vladivostock, January* 5, 1919.

FOLLOWING from British consul, Ekaterinburg, of 3rd January:—

"Have just returned from Perm after taken by Siberian Army under General Peplief. Tremendous booty was captured, including 4,000 waggons, 260 locomotives, 70 per cent. of which working condition; 30,000 prisoners, 50 guns, 10 armoured cars, great number automobiles, and other material not yet counted. Part of 4,000 waggons captured full every conceivable domestic material stolen from shops and inhabitants, loaded for evacuation by Bolsheviks. Bridge across Kama intact. From interviews, local authorities and inhabitants, would appear that Bolsheviks subjected inhabitants to horrible repressions and cruelties, especially after attempt on Lenin's life. Have examined witnesses who found bodies of their relatives killed by bayonet wounds, faces wearing marks of boot nails; no bullet marks found on these bodies. Instruments used for torturing victims also found. No data available regarding number people killed; number educated people enquiring for missing male relatives stated by authorities as being very great. Educated population during last three months have been practically starving, food allowances only being given to people employed by Bolsheviks. Food supply of Bolsheviks, however, not great, one pound bad bread being allowed daily for workmen. Taking of Perm has great economic significance."

Major N.E. Reilly, I.A., Assistant Political Agent, Chitral, to the Honourable the Chief Commissioner, North-Western Frontier Province.

(Extract.)   *Chitral, January* 7, 1919.

I HAVE the honour to report that a party of Russian refugees has arrived at Mastuj.

I understand that they have sought British protection as, expecting the arrival of a Bolshevik commissioner at Kharog, they considered their lives to be in danger.

The Bolsheviks are stated to have bayonetted the brother and nephew of Captain Chkapsky, whilst I also understood from Captain Besobrazor that all his family had been murdered by Bolsheviks at Tashkent.

They state that the Bolsheviks are destroying everything, and that at Tashkent the daily allowance had been reduced to 1/4 lb. (Russian) of bread per head.

General Poole to War Office.—(Received January 9.)

(Telegraphic.)   *January* 8, 1919.

THE Bolsheviks are now employing gangs of Chinese for the purpose of killing officers and deserters. Peasants have been killed by these gangs for refusing to comply with requisitioning decrees, and even the families of officers serving here have been murdered. The above is based on authentic information.

General Poole to War Office.—(Received January 12.)

(Telegraphic.)   *January* 11, 1919.

FROM intercepted radios and leaflets it is clear that, to allay hostility abroad, Bolsheviks are conducting double campaign. Leaflets are distributed among German troops, while decrees, which are not intended to be put into force, and appeals are radioed to Berlin, which show Bolsheviks in sufficiently liberal light to bring them into line with German Socialists. Appeals to unite and force world-wide revolution are made at the same time to proletarians. It is manifest from numerous deserters and refugees from Central Russia efforts to destroy social and economic life of country have not abated.

There is evidence to show that commissariats of free love have been established in several towns, and respectable women flogged for refusing to yield. Decree for nationalisation of women has been put into force, and several experiments made to nationalise children. I trust His Majesty's Government will not allow Peace Conference to be influenced by Bolshevik presentation of their case abroad, as their action at home is diametrically opposed to this.

Mr. Alston to Mr. Balfour.—(Received January 15.)

(Telegraphic.)   *Vladivostock, January* 14, 1919.

I HAVE received following from consul at Ekaterinburg, dated the 13th January:—

"The number of innocent civilians brutally murdered in Ural towns run into hundreds. Officers taken prisoners by Bolsheviks here had their shoulder straps nailed into their shoulders, girls have been raped, some of the civilians have been found with their eyes pierced out, others without noses, whilst twenty-five priests were shot at Perm, Bishop Andronick having been buried alive there.

"I have been promised the total number of killed and other details, when available."

General Knox to War Office.—(Received January 16.)

(Telegraphic.)   *Omsk, January* 15, 1919.

AN officer has just returned from a few days' visit to Perm. Before the revolution he was employed at Perm. He states that he arrived there on the 28th December. The town was captured by the Bolsheviks on the 24th, and they fed no one except those in their employ. He says he was unable to recognise his old acquaintances, as their cheeks were sunken, their faces were yellow, and they looked like palsied old men. The Bolsheviks have raised a battalion of 700 officers, but they will have to be fed for several weeks before they are in a condition to fight. Starvation will, he says, claim half the population of the towns before June if Bolshevism is not stamped out in Russia. The peasants hate the Bolsheviks owing to constant requisitions, but they are better off. The peasants will only sow sufficient for their own needs for next harvest. He is of opinion that Bolsheviks will not be suppressed without the use of outside force, as anti-Bolshevik classes are too enfeebled by hunger to make any effort. There are of course numerous murders. There was one commissary who used to have a dozen prisoners out every night, and before loading by ball-cartridge, made the firing party snap their rifles at them ten or a dozen times.

As the educated workmen have been taken away by the Bolsheviks, the chances of the factories producing anything for several months is negligible. It is difficult to bring coal from the Ural mountains, as the bridges over the Chusovbravaya, east of Perm, have been destroyed. Is it possible that public opinion in Allied countries will allow Bolsheviks to continue this wholesale murder?

They will, moreover, increase in strength as Russians have to serve them or starve. This matter is not one that only concerns Russia, as the food supply of the world is affected.

Mr. Alston to Mr. Balfour.—(Received January 20.)

(Telegraphic.) *Vladivostock, January* 18, 1919.

I HAVE been given following information by member of Red Cross Mission, Dr. T—, who has just returned to Vladivostock from the neighbourhood of Perm. He says that for rank barbarous brutality, the horrors which he has witnessed of Bolshevik legacies in the localities which they evacuated, the tortures and mutilations performed on wounded and others before death, baffle description. Even ferocity of Turks in Armenia cannot be compared with what is now being done in Russia by Bolsheviks.

Dr. T— understands the Russian point of view, as he has been in actual contact with Bolshevism.

When I asked him to furnish more precise details, he told me it was difficult to furnish the dates, exact spots, names, &c. The report from Ekaterinburg of brutal murder of hundreds of innocent civilians at Perm, of mutilation of priests, and of tortures, such as of officers having their shoulder straps nailed into their shoulders is, however, absolutely confirmed by him.

Dr. T— found on battlefield during fighting in Usuri district in July, 1918 bodies of Czech soldiers in frightful state of mutilation, their private parts cut off, their heads cut open, their faces slashed, their eyes gouged out, and their tongues cut out. A doctor of H.M.S. "Suffolk" attended four of such cases, which were brought to Vladivostock for official investigation. These mutilations were inflicted before death, according to verdict given.

The local representative of Czech National Council, Dr. Girsa, and his assistant, state that over a year ago hundreds of officers were shot at Kief, when Bolsheviks captured that city. Premier Rodzianko was shot, and massacre of Prince Yashuisen was brutal murder. In the face of bitterest cold these men were taken from their homes and thrown into automobiles and carts, and, except for their caps, were made to strip naked. In the biting cold they were forced for hours to stand in line, and Bolshevik soldiers were given liberty of shooting them in groups or singly, as it pleased their fancy.

Dr. Girsa was surgeon in civilian hospital No. 12 at this time. This hospital was crowded with patients on account of the ruthless manner in which the Bolsheviks were attacking the more educated classes and the officers in the city of Kief. It was necessary to hide officers in closets, even when mortally wounded, to prevent Bolsheviks coming in and taking them out to be shot in the streets.

Many seriously wounded were taken from Kief hospitals and ruthlessly murdered in the streets. Bolsheviks forced into the streets and shot men with abdominal wounds, broken limbs, and grave injuries in other parts of their bodies. He recollects seeing officers being eaten by dogs in the streets of Kief. Wife of Dr. Girsa's assistant herself saw an automobile load of frozen bodies of dead officers being carried through the streets to a dumping ground outside the town.

These men were forced out of their homes in the middle of the night, hospital beds were emptied, patients who were seriously ill were ruthlessly slaughtered, and men were shot without mercy and without trial.

A surgeon in the employment of the Red Cross in Vladivostock verified these accounts. He himself saw such crimes, and fled from the vicinity of Moscow in terror with his wife. Photographs of murdered civilians were shown me.

Colonel Wade to British Peace Conference Commission, Paris, and Foreign Office.

(Telegraphic.) *Warsaw, January* 19, 1919.
NUMBER of Corean and Chinese units is reported to be increasing by persons arriving from Ukraine and Soviet Russia. Sole object of these units is plunder, as they are merely bandits and not a regular army. Gravity of situation created by this new development cannot be sufficiently emphasised.

Mr. Alston to Earl Curzon.—(Received January 25.)

(Telegraphic.) *Vladivostock, January 23, 1919.*
FOLLOWING from High Commissioner:—

"Following statements respecting Bolsheviks in Perm and neighbourhood are taken from reports sent by His Majesty's consul at Ekaterinburg. The Omsk Government have similar information:—

"The Bolsheviks can no longer be described as a political party holding extreme communistic view. They form relatively small privileged class which is able to terrorise the rest of the population because it has a monopoly both of arms and of food supplies. This class consists chiefly of workmen and soldiers, and included a large non-Russian element, such as Letts and Esthonians and Jews; the latter are specially numerous in higher posts. Members of this class are allowed complete licence, and commit crime against other sections of society.

"The army is well disciplined, as a most strict system especially is applied to it.

"It is generally said that officers are forced to serve because their families are detained as hostages. The population of Perm was rationed, and non-Bolsheviks received only $\frac{1}{4}$ lb. of bread a day.

"The peasantry suffered less, but were forbidden under pain of death to sell food to any but Bolsheviks.

"The churches were closed, for many priests were killed, and a bishop was buried alive.

"This and other barbarous punishments, such as dipping people in rivers till they were frozen to death.

"Those condemned to be shot were led out several times and fired at with blank cartridges, never knowing when the real execution would take place. Many other atrocities are reported.

"The Bolsheviks apparently were guilty of wholesale murder in Perm, and it is certain that they had begun to operate a plan of systematic extermination. On a lamp above a building were the words: 'Only those who fight shall eat.'"

Lord Kilmarnock to Earl Curzon.—(Received February 1.)

My Lord,   *Copenhagen, January* 21, 1919.
I HAVE the honour to report that a reliable Danish engineer, employed in the Ryabusinsky factory near Moscow, who has travelled considerably in Russia lately, and who left Petrograd on the 11th instant,

reports that there is a growing tendency on the part
of the Central Committees to disregard the local
committees and to absorb all the power. Though the
Bolshevik régime was more hated than ever, resistance
from inside was less strong, and as nearly the whole
population was suffering from starvation the people
were physically incapable of throwing off the yoke of
the oppressors. My informant stated that recently, in
connection with arranging a credit for his factory, he
had to deal with the committees, and he was surprised
to find how largely they were recruited from former
officers, directors of factories, &c., and he said that
every day there were fewer people who refused to
serve the Red Guard. The hostility between the soldiers and the peasants was less acute as the stocks of
the latter were now exhausted and they no longer
feared the arbitrary requisitions of the guards. Only
the smaller peasants were admitted to the committees.

The Chinese guard in Petrograd numbered about
5,000, and discipline in the Bolshevik army was
severer than ever before and executions as numerous.
Peasants were being mobilised, but as they resisted,
they were always distributed in several regiments so
that there should be no large focus of discontent in
any particular regiment.

His own factory, which had been nationalised,
was still working and 6,000 workmen were
employed. Though there were still a few Bolsheviks
among them, the majority had gradually seceded and
had given up their belief in Bolshevism. As the factory
owned a forest they were still able to get fuel, and

shoddy goods were turned out, which were handed over to the Central, but my informant states that they were not sold, but were added to the stocks of goods collected by the Central. His factory was one of the few that were still working as, owing to lack of raw materials and especially of fuel, one after another had been obliged to close down. A passenger train ran daily between Petrograd and Moscow and a few goods trains, but owing to lack of fuel it was stated that this service would be further curtailed.

As regards food conditions, the situation was getting worse day by day, and in Petrograd the majority of persons were living on 1/2–lb. of oats a day. The Red Guards were better off, as they could still obtain small quantities of tea, sugar, and bread, but even for the highest prices other people could not get food.

Transport difficulties increased day by day as there were hardly any horses left in Petrograd, and innumerable formalities had to be gone through before a parcel could be taken from a shop or a store. All transport without a permit was prohibited.

The food question dominates all others.

I have, &c.
KILMARNOCK.

Mr. Alston to Earl Curzon.—(Received February 3.)

(Telegraphic.)   *Vladivostock, February* 1, 1919.
FOLLOWING from High Commissioner, 30th January:—

"Consul at Ekaterinburg has forwarded a report from Military Investigation Commission at Verkhoturie in Northern Urals to following effect:—

"British workman, Alexander Smith, was arrested and kept in prison at Verkhoturie by Bolshevik authorities from 30th September to 12th October, 1918, on which latter day he was shot. Order for imprisonment contained no charge, and Commission state that they believe that he was arrested solely because he was a British subject.

"When Government troops occupied Verkhoturie on 16th October they found body outside the town 'in a mutilated condition,' and gave it ceremonious burial.

"I hear that Bolsheviks killed two British subjects at Perm. Names unknown."

Mr. Alston to Earl Curzon.—(Received February 3.)

(Telegraphic.)   *Vladivostock, February* 2, 1919.
FOLLOWING from High Commissioner 31st January:—

"Following details respecting Bolshevik régime at Lisva, a town of 30,000 inhabitants between Ekaterinburg and Perm, were given to me by Mr. T—, a British subject, who was there until 17th December, when the town was taken.

"Life was tolerable until July. A system of rations was in force before Bolsheviks came into power, and was not at first abused.

"Terrorism began after attempt on Lenin in July.

Considerable numbers of people were shot in Lisva and other towns for no apparent reason. Persons were arrested and had to bail themselves out often several times, and often under threats of death. Orders were received to arrest all foreigners, especially British and French. Mr. T— was able to hide, and was only under arrest for a short time.

"In the town there were 25 commissioners and 1,000 smaller officials. They drew 6,000,000 roubles salary, occupied houses of the upper and middle classes, and had plenty of provisions, as had also the soldiers.

"Non-Bolsheviks had 1/4-pound of bread per day.

"He thought wholesale murder or bodily torture was the exception, but he confirmed reports of people being led out to be shot several times. Many people went mad under this and similar mental agony.

"Churches were not closed, but soldiers were forbidden attendance, and bells were not rung. Only civil marriages were permitted. He had heard nothing about nationalisation of women.

"Army was well disciplined, and he believes it is still formidable. Officers forced to serve in it did not seem to mind their position as much as might be expected. Soldiers were allowed to loot freely. When Lisva was evacuated 1,800 prisoners were removed to Perm.

"Considered as a machine for executing its own purposes, he thought Bolshevik administration efficient and energetic. There was a regular service of trains between Urals and European Russia, but only Bolshevik officers could have passenger car, others travelling in trucks.

"Peasantry were against Bolsheviks because they were subject to unnecessary requisitions, whereas workmen had much higher wages and did much less work than formerly.

"Mr. T— said that we ought not to treat with them as a political party, and that he believed conditions of life in Petrograd and Moscow were terrible, and much worse than in Eastern Russia."

Mr. Alston to Earl Curzon.—(Received February 6.)

(Telegraphic.)   *Vladivostock, February* 4, 1919.

FOLLOWING from consul at Ekaterinburg, dated 1st February:—

"According to information received from General Staff here, prisoners returning from Germany via Vyatka report armed revolt of peasants of Vyatka district against Bolshevik mobilisation. Not only revolters themselves suffered death penalty for revolting, but also their whole families."

∞∞∞

**Interviews with Mr. A. and Mr. B., who left
Moscow on January 21, 1919.**

MR. A. and Mr. B., two British subjects who left
Moscow on the 21st January, were interviewed at the
Foreign Office on the 10th February about present
conditions in Moscow.

Mr. B., who was a teacher in a Moscow secondary
school, the "practical academy," gave the following
information about conditions in the school in which
he taught. This school was typical of many others.

Each class has its committee, and as a rule the

most popular boy is chosen to represent the others at the masters' meetings. The objects of the committees are: (1) to control the masters; (2) to arrange about the distribution of food, all the boys and girls in the school being given a mid-day meal. This is, as a matter of fact, the only reason that they go to school at all.

Both boys and girls are herded together, and there is no semblance of morality. The entire absence of discipline in this connection is having an extremely bad effect on the coming generation. In the classes all semblance of discipline has been destroyed. The children do exactly as they like, sometimes walking out in the middle of a lesson. This is especially the case in the lesson before the mid-day meal, as they are all anxious to get the first places. No punishments, no homework and no marks are allowed. The attendance is abominable, the children coming and going just as they think fit. It is impossible to keep order, and the classes are simply like a bear-garden. If a master does not happen to be popular, the boys turn him out. Sometimes a master may go to a class to give a lesson, only to find the boys holding a committee meeting which must not be disturbed.

At Kolomna, between Moscow and Kazan, a boy aged 18 was appointed commissar of the whole school, being in charge of all the teachers. On one occasion he closed the school for a whole week because one of the masters gave a boy a bad mark.

The universities suffer from the same lack of discipline. Any boy of 16 years of age is entitled to enter the university without showing any certificate, so that even if a boy is unable to read or write, he can still enter the university.

The Bolsheviks have advertised far and wide the benefits of the new proletarian culture. The above facts throw an interesting light on the way it works in practice.

Mr. A., who is a Moscow man, gave the following information about: (1) the "terror"; (2) conditions in factories with which he was acquainted; (3) the shops in Moscow:—

1. *The "Terror."*

Executions still continue in the prisons, though the ordinary people do not hear about them. Often during the executions a regimental band plays lively tunes. The following account of an execution was given to Mr. A. by a member of one of the bands. On one occasion he was playing in the band, and as usual all the people to be executed were brought to the edge of the grave. Their hands and feet were tied together so that they would fall forward into the grave. They were then shot through the neck by Lettish soldiers. When the last man had been shot the grave was closed up, and on this particular occasion the band-man saw the grave moving. Not being able to stand the sight of it, he fainted, whereupon the Bolsheviks seized him, saying that he was in sympathy with the prisoners. They were on the point of killing him, but other members of the band explained that he was really ill, and he was then let off.

Among the prisoners shot on that occasion was a priest, who asked permission to say a prayer before being shot, to which the Bolsheviks replied laconically, "Ne Nado" (It is not necessary).

2. *Conditions in Factories.*

At the principal factory at Kolomna, a town on the Moscow and Kazan Railway, there are only about 5,000 workers out of the normal total of 25,000. The factory is run by a committee of three—one workman, one engineer, and one director. Here, as everywhere, all the workmen are discontented and would much prefer the old management. The situation is intolerable. Nobody works and nobody wants to work, while the one and only topic of conversation is food. All the people are discontented because they have not got enough to eat.

At Domodedova, near Moscow, the fine-cloth factory was still working before Christmas, but the output was estimated at 5 per cent. of the normal. The factory was run by a Committee of Workmen, but the owner used to meet the Committee occasionally to discuss the working of the factory with them, and to give them advice. All the workmen were discontented with the way in which the factory was run, and most of them wanted the old managers back again. But as long as the Bolsheviks pay the men high wages they will stay there, though they do practically no work at all. They have to pretend to be Bolshevik, but in reality they are not in sympathy with them at all.

3. *Shops in Moscow.*

No shops are open at all except the Soviet shops. The Bolsheviks close down certain shops, take down the signs, and remove all the material without paying for it. They then put up signs of their own announcing the sale of clothing, which they sell at twice the price which was charged at the shop from which they took the stuff. No new stuff is now being made at all. What is now being sold is entirely old stock.

Lord Kilmarnock to Earl Curzon.

My Lord,   *Copenhagen, February* 3, 1919.
I HAVE the honour to report that a French gentle-
man, who left Petrograd towards the end of January,
has given me the following information as regards the
situation in Russia:—

M. F— was of opinion that the military and civil
power of the Bolsheviks had reached its zenith and
was already on the decline. The leaders of the movement had acquired strength, first because they held
out prospects of limitless pillaging to their followers,

and then by reserving for the Red Guard the remaining supplies of food. These supplies were now exhausted, and the money which was so lavishly given to the Guards could buy nothing. When the workmen were discontented in the past, the Bolsheviks had been able to quell disorder by making a distribution of flour, but now they could offer nothing to the workmen except depreciated roubles. The lack of arms and ammunition was becoming serious, and the frequent desertions, especially of the peasant soldiers, had a demoralising effect on the army.

The Bolsheviks comprised chiefly Jews and Germans, who were exceedingly active and enterprising. The Russians were largely anti-Bolshevik, but were for the most part dreamers, incapable of any sustained action, who now, more than ever before, were unable to throw off the yoke of their oppressors. Night after night the counter-revolutionary Societies held secret meetings to plot against the Bolsheviks, but never once was a serious attempt made to carry through the conspiracy. The starving condition of the people quite paralysed their will-power.

The country was in a complete state of anarchy. When Petrograd said "yes," Moscow said "no," and neither was able to impose their will on the local Soviets in the provinces, though the Soviet at Moscow especially was endeavouring to establish its hold over all the country. There were no newspapers except those printed in Moscow, which were full of lies; railway communications were coming to an end, and strikes were of frequent occurrence. In Petrograd practically all the factories were idle, and in the Moscow district but few were still working; and as an example of the commercial apathy into which the country had sunk, M. F— mentioned that the famous Putilov works had only turned out one engine in a whole month. The committees of the poor paralysed all trade, which was further hampered by increasing local jealousies, and it was now practically impossible to move goods or fuel from one quarter to another, or even from one house to another. The interference of these committees had led to such a state that the peasants had refused to bring food in to the cities, but preferred to bury their small stocks; and though lately the situation had slightly improved, the position was precarious and he could not see how the population of Northern Russia would survive the months of February, March, and April. Fortunately the weather had so far been mild, as no fuel was available. He himself had managed to live on biscuits and sardines, but when he left Petrograd people had to exist on about half a pound of oats a day. At any moment even the supply of oats might be exhausted.

He said that the Bolshevik leaders felt that their days were numbered, and they were trying to introduce into the direction of affairs representatives of the more moderate parties, such as the Revolutionary Socialists, and their programme was being modified accordingly. The "Terrorism" had lately been less severe, the executions fewer, and many of the Red Guards themselves were being shot on account of the crimes which they had committed. An effort was being made to carry out the principles of "communism" on a more ideal basis, and though there was no effective restraint on plundering and thieving on the part of the Red Guards, still it happened now that selfish thieves, *i.e.*, thieves who stole and refused to share the booty with the other Guards, were shot by their comrades. M. F— was quite positive, however, that the interesting experiment of introducing "communism" had definitely failed.

Any régime which could offer food to the people would at once gain their support, and any régime, however tyrannical and however corrupt, would be milder and more honest than the present.

I have, &c.,

KILMARNOCK.

Mr. Alston to Earl Curzon.—(Received February 11.)

(Telegraphic.)   *Vladivostock, February* 8, 1919.

FOLLOWING from consul at Ekaterinburg, 6th February:—

"From examination of several labourer and peasant witnesses I have evidence to the effect that very smallest percentage of this district were pro-Bolshevik, majority of labourers sympathising with summoning of Constituent Assembly. Witnesses further stated that Bolshevik leaders did not represent Russian working classes, most of them being Jews.

"As a result of refusal of 4,000 labourers near Ekaterinburg to support local Bolsheviks many were arrested, and twelve were suffocated alive in slag gas-pit, their mutilated bodies being buried afterwards, and ninety peasants taken out of Ekaterinburg prison, where they had been thrown because they objected to Bolsheviks requisitioning their cattle, &c., were brutally murdered."

Sir H. Rumbold to Earl Curzon.

My Lord,   *Berne, February* 5, 1919.

I HAVE the honour to transmit to your Lordship herewith a copy of a letter addressed by Madame X——, a Polish lady, from Cracow, to a compatriot at Paris.

Madame X——'s letter gives a certain amount of apparently first-hand information relative to conditions in the Ukraine, where, according to the writer, the Poles have frequently been the victims of appalling outrages.

I have, &c.
HORACE RUMBOLD.

Enclosure
Letter from Madame X——.

(Translation.)

Dear——,   *Cracow, January* 17, 1919.

I OFTEN wonder if you and our fellow-country-men in Switzerland know anything about the events which are occurring in the unfortunate parts of our country from which we were forced to flee. I imagine very little is known, and yet these regions, although far from the centre, are nevertheless in Europe, and are still inhabited by civilised people, who are at present in the most terrible state. Their property is confiscated and pillaged, their lives are often in danger, and they cannot even flee, as their retreat is cut off.

From October 1917 to February 1918 bands of soldiers and armed peasants pillaged and laid waste the whole of Russia and the Ukraine; all household property without exception—farms, gentlemen's places, and buildings of every description—were burnt or pulled down, forests cut down, without any-one in authority putting an end to this craze for destruction. This is the way the Russian and Ukrainian peasants entered into possession of the lands granted them freely by the Bolshevik Government and the Ukrainian Government. It is needless to add that nothing escaped being pillaged, not even churches and graves being spared. The unfortunate landed proprietors, as well the farmers, farm labourers, and workmen in factories took refuge in the towns in an attempt to save what they could of their belongings. There pillaging still continued, on the plea of carrying out a search. The arrival of the Austro-German armies in February 1918 put an end to this craze for robbery and rapine.

Owners regained possession of their property, of the ruins of their houses and farms, and what remained of their forests. There was even mention of a commission which would make a valuation of losses suffered and make those responsible pay for them.

However, in the winter of 1918 the Austro-German armies retreated, and a band of bravoes resumed the reins of Government in the Ukraine, and the land became again the prey of peasants' committees, who cannot pillage anything, as the country is laid waste and covered with ruins.

What is happening now is of quite a different nature, and is manifestly anti-Polish. Last year it was landed proprietors that were attacked, now they want to destroy everything Polish regardless of class distinctions.

As I am far away and have little news, my information is certainly somewhat meagre, and yet the events that I am going to relate to you are true.

In the Proskorow district the peasants burnt M. Stanislas Skibiewski alive after torturing him for two days. Two brothers Kostkiewiez, as well as Mme. Malinowska, were murdered by peasants. Mme. Marie Mankowska and her son have been imprisoned for several weeks, and nobody knows what will happen to them. All the prisons are crammed with Poles who are undergoing the most terrible treatment. Jerome Sobanski and his son are among the prisoners.

Fourteen members of Michel Sobanski's Government were frightfully tortured before being killed, and the same fate has befallen the members of Bialo Cerkiew's Government. At Brycow seven members of the Grocholsey Government were mutilated before being murdered. In Berdiozew district Malaszewski, manager of a factory, and Wroezynski, sub-manager, were murdered. In Volhynia the two brothers Plater of Dambrovica were burnt alive. At Kamieneo, Alexandre Sadowski has been in prison for a long time, and great anxiety is felt for his life. At Czere Paszynce the gamekeeper was killed after being frightfully tortured. Catholic priests are exposed to every indignity, and their lives are always in danger. At Bazalia during Mass seventy people were arrested in church. In the towns Polish and Russian landowners are arrested and imprisoned. The peasants in the country come to find them, and the prisoners are handed over to them with permission to do what they like with them. It is only by means of very heavy ransoms that they manage occasionally to save their lives.

With regard to your own property, the house and the farmhouses were still standing last November. Malejowce is destroyed, and the forests are in a terrible state. At Strychowce nothing is left standing; our properties are completely laid waste.

Petlura's band has seized the banks as well as the sugar factories, and it is impossible to draw any money or shares belonging to companies without first obtaining the signature of the peasants' committee.

It is also said that half the money in the banks belonging to private accounts has been confiscated. At any rate, it is quite certain that part of the capital belonging to private individuals has been seized at the Union Bank at Kamisnec.

If public opinion, as voiced by the European press, has denounced and condemned the excesses and crimes committed in Belgium, Serbia, and the

Duchy of Posen, why should the crimes committed by the Bolsheviks and the Ukrainians remain unknown? It is the wish of the unfortunate people who ask for the assistance and implore the protection of the Allied armies, that France, England, and America should be informed of what is going on.

As Warsaw turns a deaf ear, being too much taken up with its political questions, and the Polish armies have enough to do with the Ruthenians in Galicia, and cannot give any help to people further away, we should like our committees in Switzerland to be kept fully informed, and to be able to represent to the French and English press how matters stand. It is with this object in view that I write to you and place myself at your disposal if more information can be sent which could be published in the press.

✻

Lord Kilmarnock to Earl Curzon.—(Received February 11.)

My Lord,   *Copenhagen, February* 6, 1919.

I HAVE the honour to forward herewith a translation of the first official report on the atrocities committed by the Bolsheviks in Wesenberg and Dorpat, which has been furnished me by the Esthonian representative here.

I have, &c.
KILMARNOCK.

Enclosure

ATROCITIES PERPETRATED BY THE BOLSHEVIKS IN ESTHONIA.

In Wesenberg.

AFTER the Esthonian troops had reconquered the town of Wesenberg from the Bolsheviks, the graves of those murdered by the latter during their short period of "terrorism" were opened on the 17th January, 1919. The following officials were present: Town Governor, Aren; President of the District Administration, Hr. Juhkam; Deputy Mayor, Jakobson; Militia Commandant, Kütt; Assistant Militia Commandant, Tenneberg; Medical Officer of Health, Dr. Wiren; and the previous Medical Officer of Health, Dr. Utt.

The vicinity of the graves of the victims to the Red Terror showed with what brutal roughness the Bolsheviks had executed their victims. Everywhere was to be seen congealed blood amongst which tattered pieces of cap, bits of clothing, brains, and fragments of skull with hair could be distinguished. In the first grave sixteen bodies were found, which were later photographed. Among these the following were identified: Army doctor, Dr. Reinik; the Greek Catholic priest, Sergei Filorenski; ambulance soldier, Ellenberg, of Reval; the local merchant, Gustav Bock; Tönis Pödra, of Gut Uhtna; a railway official, Tönu Pöiklik, of Wesenberg; Ferdinand Tops, from the parish of Undle; Rudolf Rost, ambulance soldier, of Tudulinne; Ednard Sepp, of the Estate Welsi; and the shoemaker Kolk, of Wesenberg. Sixteen victims were also in the other grave. The following were recognised: Heinrich Mikker, of Kunda; Joh. Ed. Järw, of Gem Küti; Juri Juhkam, of the parish of Roela; Hugo Lang, of the parish of Küti; Josep Koovits, of Kunda; Harriette von Mühlen, of the Tudu Estate; Walter Pauker, the clergyman of Wesenberg; Gustav Sone, from the parish of Küti; von Hesse, an official of Wesenberg; Peter Sakkar, from Kunda; Arthur Sulto, from Kunda; Jakob Raja, forester from the Estate of Lobu; Hugo Rannaberg, from the parish of Küti.

The third and largest of the graves was opened on the 18th January. It was 4 metres long and 2 metres deep, and filled to the top with corpses. Fifty bodies were found here, among whom the following were recognised: Rudolf Peets, of Laekwere; Carl Erde, of Haljala; Daniel Sellow, a merchant of Laekwere; Jean Rebane, from the village of Assanalls; Johannes Lomberg, of Ambla; Hindrick Roosilill, from the Tape Estate; Eduard Walow, of Wesenberg; Gustav Koolmann, of Walnupea; Mihkel Klein, from the parish of Küti; August Marton, from Malla; Dr. Morits Ling, from Kunda; Siim Magi, of Malla; Juri Kuller, from the Inju Estate; Johannes Marton, from Malla; Konrad Preisberg, of Ambla; Ernst Klein, from the parish of Küti; Karl Paas, of Kuline; Arthur Wään, soldier of the Militia, from the parish of Wihula; Jüri Lemming, of Ambla; Willen Püdermann, of Rahkla; Karl Knanf, proprietor of Nomkula; Karl Pudel, from Rahkla; Johannes Schmitnar, tenant of the Tapa Estate; Frau van Rehekampf, of Wesenberg; August

Paas, of Kulina; Lüna Lümann, of the parish of Aaspere; Jeannette, Baroness Wrangel, of Wesenberg; Frau von Samson, of Wesenberg; Leopold Aron, head of the Post Stage of Wesenberg; Jaan Paas, of Kulina; railway official Older, of St. Püssi; Mihkel Marton, of Malla; Jüri Magi, of Inju; Feodar Nümm, of Osel; Bernh. Wold Lessel, of Wesenberg; Masik, soldier of the people's army from the Government of Twer; J. Heinrich Grauberg, of Rahkla; Prüdik Wilder, of Laekwere; Julius Kütsel, of Laekwere; Marta Afanasjewa, Sister of Mercy, of Kunda; Marie Kirsch, of Wesenberg.

All the bodies showed signs of the rage and revenge of the Bolsheviks. The victims were all robbed of everything except their linen, their boots also having been taken. The Bolsheviks had shattered the skulls of thirty-three of the bodies, so that the heads hung like bits of wood on the trunks. As well as being shot, most of the murdered had been pierced with bayonets, the entrails torn out, and the bones of the arm and leg broken.

How the victims were executed by the Bolsheviks is described by one of these unfortunates, Proprietor A. Munstrum, who managed to save himself by a miracle:—

"On the afternoon of the 11th January, fifty-six of us were led to the place of execution, where the grave was already made. Half of us, including six women, were placed at the edge of the grave. The women were to be killed first, as their cries were so heartrending the murderers could not listen to them any longer. One woman tried to escape, but did not get far. They fired a volley, and she sank to the ground wounded. Then the Bolsheviks dragged her by the feet into the grave. Five of the murderers sprang after her, shot at her, and stamped on her body with their feet till she was silent. Then a further volley was fired at the other victims. In the same way they were thrown into the graves and done to death with butt-ends and bayonets. After which the murderers once more stamped on the bodies ..."

In Dorpat.

ALSO in Dorpat the Bolsheviks committed the same kind of atrocities as in Wesenberg. On Christmas evening the well-known Director of Fisheries, Zoological Student Max von zur Mühlen, was murdered.

On the 26th December the following persons were shot: Mihkel Küs, Alex Lepp, Alexander Aland, and Karl Soo.

On the 9th January the Bolsheviks murdered the following persons: August Meos, Abram Schreiber, Woldemar Rästa, butcher Beer Stark, Baron Paul von Tiesenhausen, Woldemar and Johann Ottas, Mikhel Kure, Friedrich Päss, Bruno von Samson-Himmelstjerna, Harald von Samson-Himmelstjerna, Gustav von Samson-Himmelstjerna, goldsmith Rudolf Kipasto.

All these persons were dragged to the Embach River and shot down. The dead bodies were put into the river through ice-holes. Later, when the Esthonian troops had reconquered Dorpat, sixteen of these victims of the Red Terror were found in the Embach. As could be ascertained from the bodies, these victims had been tortured in the most dreadful manner. Many had arms and legs broken, the skull knocked in, &c. It was evident that Karl Soo, who was shot on the 26th December, had suffered most of all. The Bolsheviks had put out his eyes. On the 14th January, shortly before they were driven out by the Esthonian troops, the Bolsheviks killed twenty of their prisoners. After an official enquiry it was ascertained that this bloody deed took place in the following manner: the poor unfortunates, over 200 in number, who were kept in the Credit-system Bank and the police station, had to stand in a row. The names of the victims were then called out. They were robbed of their clothes, boots, and valuables, and led to the cellar of the Credit-system Bank, where the Bolsheviks, with hatchet blows, shattered their skulls. In this manner the above-mentioned, approximately twenty persons, were murdered, and only the hasty flight of the Red Guard from the Esthonian troops saved the remaining prisoners, among whom were from sixty to eighty women. Otherwise they would have been done to death in the same way. Among the bodies of the murdered the following were recognised: Archbishop Platon; Recording Clerk Michael Bleiwe, of the Unspenski Church; the grey-headed clergyman of the Greek Orthodox Georgs-Church; Priest Nikoli Beshanitzki; Professor and University clergyman Dr. Traugott Hahu; Hermann von Samson-Himmelstjerna, of Kawershof; Heinrich von Krasse, owner of Rewold; Banker Arnold von Tideböhl, Herbert von Schrenk, Baron Konstant von Knorring, Pastor Wilhelm Schwartz, Councillor Gustav Tensmann, Councillor Gustav Seeland, Merchant Surman Kaplan, Master Potter Ado Luik, Merchant Harry Vogel, Merchant Massal, and co-worker of "Postimees," Kärner.

Dr. Wolfgang, of Reyher, who shortly after the murders—the bodies were still warm—examined the above-mentioned cellar of the Credit-system Bank, reports the following with regard to the appearance of the room where this foul deed took place: "The floor of the whole room was covered with bodies, piled one upon the other in most unnatural positions, which could only be attributable to a violent death. In the middle the bodies were in three layers, wearing only underclothing. Nearly all had shots in the head, which had been received recently, because in a few cases the skull had been totally shattered, and in one case the skull hung by a thread. Some bodies showed signs of several shots. All was thick with blood; also on the bed and on the walls congealed masses of blood and pieces of skull were to be seen. I counted twenty-three bodies, but it was easy to make a mistake, as it was difficult to recognise individual bodies in the heap. Not a bit of the floor was clear, so that I had to trample over bodies to reach others. The search for a sign of life was in vain."

After a later examination of the bodies, it was found that Bishop Platon had a bullet in the brain over the right eye, and death had been instantaneous. The left side of Priest Bleiwe's face had been shattered from the blow of an axe. The Bolshevik executioner's axe had hit Priest Bjeschanitzki in the middle of his face. From these blows the faces of both priests were so mutilated as to be almost beyond recognition. Both the arms and the head of Vicar Schwartz were hacked off. The Bolsheviks had nailed an officer's shoulder straps firmly to his shoulders. All the bodies and the cellar where they lay have been photographed.

o·•◊◊◊•·o

**Mr. Alston to Earl Curzon.—(Received
February 12.)**

(Telegraphic.) *Vladivostock, February* 11, 1919.
I HAVE received the following statement from a
British consular official, who was at Ekaterinburg in
September, 1918, regarding the situation in that town
during Bolshevik régime, from 1917 until the end of
1918, when town was relieved by Czechs:—

"Bolsheviks ruthlessly 'nationalised' all property
during first four or five months, including British
firms, like Contutshtim, Syssert, &c., and they made

constant demands on all moneyed merchant classes for huge contributions, with penalty of arrest and confiscation of all belongings unless paid promptly. Businesses of all kinds, banks, and houses were either placed under control of labour elements or nationalised, and to such a low level were industry and manufacture reduced that they practically came to a standstill. Systematic searches of houses and private individuals took place daily, and gold and silver ornaments, and even spare clothes, were taken without compensation, and merchants who attempted to resist or evade constant decrees from local Soviet were immediately arrested. Robberies and murders were frequent, law and order were at very low ebb, and almost complete anarchy reigned. A local consular corps was formed in March, 1918, consisting of consuls and representatives of some dozen different nationalities to act as an intermediary between Bolshevik Soviet and subjects of foreign Powers, owing to the molestation of foreign subjects.

"All public meetings were suppressed, and, with the exception of the daily official organ of the Bolsheviks, no papers or printed matter could be published.

"Czech movement on Omsk began towards the end of May. We were in a state of siege from the end of May to the 25th July, when Bolsheviks finally evacuated the town and Czechs marched in. Bolshevik terrorism succeeded Bolshevik despotism. Having publicly announced their intention of making "red terror" as dreadful as possible, they arrested hundreds of private citizens as hostages for the sole reason that they belonged to so-called bourgeoisie and "Intelligentsia." Hotels and private residences were requisitioned to accommodate these hostages, as prisons were full of them; under armed bands of Red Guards scores were taken to the front to do work for "Proletariat Army," and dig trenches. Without semblance of a trial, many of them were shot during June and July. A placard on the walls of one of the gates which was reprinted in Bolshevik paper the following day, was the first intimation we had of this. This proclamation gave names of nineteen citizen hostages who had been shot, amongst whom were the member of a well-known engineering firm, Mr. Fadyef, and the manager of Syssert Company (an English undertaking), Mr. Makronosoef. The rest were mostly peaceful hard-working merchants and mostly well-known persons. Eight more were shot a few days later, amongst them being the son of a wealthy flour-miller, Mr. Markarow. Number of bodies, amounting, I believe, to sixty or more, were discovered after Czechs took the town. Subsequently it was discovered that they were shot in the most cruel manner, just like animals in woods, and some of them were undoubtedly left to die on the ground, as no pains were taken to discover whether their wounds were mortal or not. It was alleged by Bolsheviks that to prevent any counter-revolutionary movement in the town it was necessary to terrorise population in this manner. Consular corps were informed roughly that Bolsheviks would allow no interference, when they protested against these wholesale assassinations. Although they vigorously denied it, Bolsheviks began to evacuate Ekaterinburg about the middle of July. One of their leaders publicly stated that if they were obliged to leave the town they would massacre a thousand citizens.

"Three days before they finally left Ekaterinburg, Bolsheviks announced at a public meeting on 25th December, that they had recently shot the Emperor. Their system of espionage was very perfect, and during whole of their régime nobody dared to utter a word that might be construed into anti-Bolshevism, as they were liable to be immediately arrested and shot.

"In addition to the above-mentioned horrors we were always anticipating an outbreak of typhus, cholera or other epidemic, as everything was in a state of unutterable filth, no attempts being made to clean buildings, offices, streets, railway stations or trains.

"Everybody appeared dejected and depressed, and decent and cleanly dressed people were seldom seen in the streets.

"Bolshevik evacuation was most thoroughly carried out, and it is estimated that they took with them over 4,000,000,000 roubles worth of platinum, gold, stores and money. There is no doubt that there would have been a great many more murders if they had not been so busily engaged in this plunder, but owing to rapid advance of Czechs, they were forced to hasten their departure.

"There will be wholesale massacres of moneyed and merchant classes if Bolsheviks succeed in retaking Ekaterinburg.

Notes on Interviews with Mr. C. and Mr. D., February 13, 1919.

MR. C. and Mr. D. were interviewed this morning in the Foreign Office. They both left Petrograd on the 17th January. Mr. C. was manager of a big firm in Petrograd, and was in prison three and a half months.

In the cities the cry of the Bolsheviks has been "the proletariat against the bourgeoisie," though as most of the big capitalists got away, it has really been the oppression of the de-bourgeoisie and the intelligent workmen by the dregs of the population.

1. *The Villages.*

In the villages poverty committees, composed of peasants without land and of hooligans returned from the towns, have been set against the peasant proprietor. Local government has been handed over to these poverty committees, and they take from the peasant proprietor his produce, implements, and live-stock, retaining what they need themselves and forwarding the remainder to the towns. The peasant will not give grain to the Bolsheviks because he hates them, and hopes by this means to destroy them eventually. He is armed and united. It is for this reason that armed requisitioning companies are sent out everywhere from Petrograd and Moscow to help the poverty committees to take the grain from the peasant, and every day all over Russia such fights for grain are fought to a finish till either the peasants or the requisitioning party are wiped out. During my stay in prison I met and talked to dozens of peasant proprietors arrested on the charge of counter-revolution. In my escape across the frontier, I slept in two peasants' cabins, and although they were living under the worst conditions, so poor that fourteen people lived and slept in a cabin a few yards square, they cursed the Bolsheviks with tears in their eyes. One of the latest decrees only allows a peasant to have one cow and one horse for every five members of his family. The peasant proprietors, who probably will one day be the strongest party in the future Russia, are anti-Bolshevik to a man.

2. *Red Army.*

No more satisfied are the soldiers. In fact the only troops the Bolsheviks can trust are the Lettish, Chinese, and a few battalions of sailors. They give them 250 roubles a month, all found, together with presents of gold watches and chains requisitioned from the bourgeoisie. Newly conscripted troops are not given rifles in Petrograd, except a few in each regiment for the purposes of instruction. They are only handed out to them at the front. For any military offence there is only one punishment—death. Executions are done mostly by the Chinese. If a regiment retreats against orders machine-guns are turned on them, and if the commissar of the regiment cannot thus hold his men he is shot. All the soldiers I spoke to, even those acting as our guards at the prison, cursed their fate at being compelled to serve, the only alternative being death from hunger or execution as deserters. Nearly all openly expressed the hope that the British would soon come and put an end to it all.

3. *Workmen.*

The position of the workmen is no better. At first the eight-hour day with high minimum wages greatly pleased them, but as time went on they found that owing to increased cost of living, they were little, if any, better off. Their wages were increased, but a vicious circle was soon set up on which their wage increases were utterly unable to keep up with the high cost of living. Reduction of output further increased the cost. At the Petrograd wagon works the pre-Bolshevik cost of passenger cars was 16,000 to 17,000 roubles; it is now 100,000 to 120,000. At Government works, where the Bolsheviks would be most likely to expect support, intense dissatisfaction exists. An official warning was issued to the workmen of the Putilof works through the official newspaper, stating that during a period of several weeks fires, explosions, and break-downs had regularly occurred, which could only be put down to traitors to the cause, who, when caught, would be shot.

4. *Bourgeoisie.*

The position of the bourgeoisie defies all description. All who employ labour down to a servant girl, or an errand boy, or anyone whose wants are provided for ahead, that is, all who do not live from hand to mouth, are considered under Bolshevism as bourgeoisie. All newspapers except the Bolshevik ones have been closed, and their plant and property confiscated. New decrees by the dozen are printed daily in the press, no other notification being given. Non-observance of any decree means confiscation of all property. All Government securities have been annulled and all others confiscated. Safe deposits have been opened, and all gold and silver articles confiscated. All plants and factories have been nationalised, as also the cinemas and theatres. This nationalisation or municipalisation means to the unhappy owner confiscation, since no payment is ever made. Payments by the banks from current or deposit accounts have been stopped. It is forbidden to sell furniture or to move it from one house to another without permission. Persons living in houses containing more rooms than they have members of their families have poor families billeted in the other rooms, the furniture in these rooms remaining for the use of the families billeted there. Hundreds of houses have been requisitioned for official or semi-official use, and thousands of unhappy residents have been turned out on the streets at an hour's notice with permission to take with them only the clothes they stood in, together with one change of linen. Houses are controlled by a poverty committee, composed of the poorest residents of the house. These committees have the right to take and distribute amongst themselves from the occupiers of the flats all furniture they consider in excess. They also act as Bolshevik agents, giving information as to movements. A special tax was levied on all house property amounting practically to the full value of the same. Failure to pay in fourteen days resulted in municipalisation of property. All owners and managers of works, offices, and shops, as well as members of the leisured classes, have been called up for compulsory labour, first for the burial of cholera and typhus victims, and later for cleaning the streets, &c. All goods lying at the custom house warehouses have been seized and first mortgaged to the Government Bank for 100,000,000 roubles. Any fortunate owner of these goods, which were not finally confiscated, had the possibility of obtaining them on payment of the mortgage. All furniture and furs stored away have been confiscated. All hotels, restaurants, provision shops, and most other shops, are now closed after having had their stocks and inventories confiscated.

Just before we left a new tax was brought out, the extraordinary Revolutionary Tax. In the Government newspapers there were printed daily lists of people, street by street, district by district, with the amount they must pay into the Government bank within fourteen days on pain of confiscation of all property. The amounts, I noticed, ranged from 2,000 roubles to 15,000,000. It is impossible to imagine how these sums can be paid.

5. *Food Question.*
The food question in Petrograd has gone from bad to worse. Elaborate food cards are given out each month covering all kinds of products, but for months past nothing has been given out on them except bread, which has for the last few weeks consisted of unmilled oats. There are now only three categories of food cards, the first being for heavy workers, the second for workers, and the third for non-workers. The last time bread was given out the daily allowance on card one was half-a-pound, on card two quarter-pound, and on card three one-eight pound. Hundreds of people are dying weekly from hunger, which first causes acute swelling of the features. Many have managed to get away, so that the present population is probably not more than 600,000. Wholesale starvation has only been prevented by the large, illicit trade done in provisions by what are

known as sack-men, who travel by rail or road from the village with food in sacks. Butter is now 80 roubles a pound; beef 25 roubles; pork 50 roubles; black bread 25 roubles; and eggs 5 roubles each. Dog-meat costs 5 roubles a pound, and horse-meat 18 roubles. Houses with central heating are no longer heated owing to lack of coal. The amount of wood that formerly cost 7 roubles, now costs 450, and only enough can be obtained for one room. Restaurants have all been confiscated and turned into communal kitchens, where the sole menu lately has been soup consisting of water with a few potatoes in it, and a herring.

6. *Oppression of Socialist Parties.*

The political parties which have been most oppressed by the Bolsheviks are the Socialists, Social Democrats, and Social Revolutionaries. Owing to bribery and corruption—those notorious evils of the old régime which are now multiplied under Bolshevism—capitalists were able to get their money from the banks and their securities from safe deposits, and managed to get away. On the other hand, many members of Liberal and Socialist parties who have worked all their time for the revolution, have been arrested or shot by the Bolsheviks. In prison I met a Social Democrat who had been imprisoned for eleven years in Schlusselberg Fortress as a political offender. Released at the beginning of the Revolution he was within eighteen months impris-oned by the Bolsheviks as a counter-revolutionary.

7. *How do the Bolsheviks Continue to hold Power?*

They continue to hold power by a system of terrorism and tyranny that has never before been heard of. This is centred at Gorokovaya 2, under the title of the Extraordinary Commission for Combating Counter-Revolution, Speculation, and Sabotage. Originally under the direction of Yourelski, it confined its operations to dealing with offences under these headings, but after his death it came out frankly as an instrument of the Red Terror, and since then its operations make the history of the French Reign of Terror, or the Spanish Inquisition, appear mild by comparison. People were arrested wholesale, not merely on individual orders on information received from spies, but literally wholesale—people arrested in the streets, theatres, cafés, every day in hundreds, and conveyed to Gorokovaya 2. There their names and other details were entered up, and next day parties of a hundred or so marched to one or another of the prisons, whilst their unhappy relations stood for hours and days in queues endeavouring to learn what had become of them. They were kept in prison two, three, or four months without any examination or accusation being made. Then some were accused and shot, fined, or all property confiscated. Others were allowed to be ransomed by their friends; others were released without any explanation. No trial was given. The accusation and examination were made together, and the examiner was generally an ex-workman, or even criminal. Examination was made in private. Sentence was confirmed by a member of the

Commission, and that is the only trial anyone ever received at Gorokovaya 2. The climax was reached after the murder of Uritsky—attack on the British Embassy, and the Lockhart affair, where hundreds of people were arrested in various parts of the town, mostly officers, who were shot and thrown into the river, bound and thrown into the river, or bound, put into barges, and the barges sunk, all without even the formality of being taken to Gorokovaya 2.

I was in prison from the 19th September to the 25th December, and I could pretty well fill a book with my experiences, but I will merely give a translation of an article printed in a Bolshevik paper, the "Northern Commune," No. 170, dated the 4th December, 1918:—

"It is impossible to continue silent. It has constantly been brought to the knowledge of the Viborg Soviet (Petrograd) of the terrible state of affairs existing in the city prisons. That people all the time are dying there of hunger; that people are detained six and eight months without examination, and that in many cases it is impossible to learn why they have been arrested, owing to officials being changed, departments closed, and documents lost. In order to confirm, or otherwise, these rumours, the Soviet decided to send on the 3rd November a commission consisting of the President of the Soviet, the district medical officer, and district military commissar, to visit and report on the "Crest" prison. Comrades! What they saw and what they heard from the imprisoned is impossible to describe. Not only were all rumours confirmed, but conditions were actually found much worse than had been stated. I was pained and ashamed. I myself was imprisoned under Tsardom in that same prison. Then all was clean, and prisoners had clean linen twice a month. Now, not only are prisoners left without clean linen, but many are even without blankets, and, as in the past, for a trifling offence they are placed in solitary confinement in cold, dark cells. But the most terrible sights we saw were in the sick bays. Comrades, there we saw living dead who hardly had strength enough to whisper their complaints that they were dying of hunger.

"In one word, amongst the sick a corpse had lain for several hours, whose neighbour managed to murmur, 'of hunger he died, and soon of hunger we shall all die.' Comrades, amongst them are many who are quite young, who wish to live and see the sunshine. If we really possess a workmen's government such things should not be."

8. *Bolshevik Plans for World Revolution.*
Bolshevism in Russia offers to our civilisation no less a menace than did Prussianism, and until it is as ruthlessly destroyed we may expect trouble, strikes, revolutions everywhere. The German military party are undoubtedly working hand in hand with Russian Bolsheviks with the idea of spreading Bolshevism ultimately to England, by which time they hope to have got over it themselves, and to be in a position to take advantage of our troubles. For Bolshevik propa-

ganda unlimited funds are available. No other country can give their secret service such a free hand, and the result is that their agents are to be found where least expected.

General Knox to War Office.

(Telegraphic.)   *Omsk, February* 5, 1919.

WITH regard to the murder of Imperial family at Ekaterinburg, there is further evidence to show that there were two parties in the local Soviet, one which was anxious to save Imperial family, and the latter, headed by five Jews, two of whom were determined to have them murdered. These two Jews, by name Vainen and Safarof, went with Lenin when he made a journey across Germany. On pretext that Russian guard had stolen 70,000 roubles, they were removed from the house between the 8th and 12th. The guard were replaced by a house guard of thirteen, consisting of ten Letts and three Jews, two of whom were called Laipont and Yurowski, and one whose name is not known. The guard was commanded outside the house by a criminal called Medoyedof who had been convicted of murder and arson in 1906, and of outraging a girl of five in 1911. The prisoners were awakened at 2 AM., and were told they must prepare for a journey. They were called down to the lower room an hour later, and Yurowski read out the sentence of the Soviet. When he had finished reading, he said, "and so your life has come to an end." The Emperor then said, "I am ready."

An eye-witness, who has since died, said that the Empress and the two eldest daughters made the sign of the cross. The massacre was carried out with revolvers. The doctor, Botkine, the maid, the valet, and the cook were murdered in this room as well as the seven members of the Imperial family. They only spared the life of the cook's nephew, a boy of fourteen. The murderers threw the bodies down the shaft of a coal mine, and the same morning orders were sent to murder the party at Alapaevsk, which was done.

Mr. Alston to Earl Curzon.—(Received February 12.)

(Telegraphic.)   *Vladivostock, February* 10, 1919.
FOLLOWING   from   consular   officer   at Ekaterinburg, 8th February:—

"From examination of witnesses of various classes of population following evidence obtained:—

"Bolsheviks persecuted all classes of population not supporting or recognising their Government. House searches, requisitions, and arrests were made at all times of day and night on grounds of political necessity, resulting in wholesale pillage. Anybody possessing more than 10,000 roubles was forced to dig trenches at front for Red Army, where they are under continual menace of death for slightest offence, and at mercy of Red Guard, very often consisting of foreigners; many of these persons were murdered. Eighteen peaceful citizens, including priests, doctors, lawyers, merchants, and labourers were arrested at Ekaterinburg as hostages, and shot without any accusations being made against them. Sixty-five citizens from Kamishlof suffered same fate. The widows of these people who claimed their husbands' bodies were treated with outrageous insult and derision by Bolsheviks. Peasants in Bolshevik district who protested against requisition of their cattle and property were thrown into prison, and ninety murdered. Peasants also had their houses burnt, as many as one hundred being destroyed in one village. Bolshevik leaders in Ekaterinburg led a life of luxury entirely in opposition to doctrine they advocated, frequently appropriating large sums of money and indulging in drunken orgies. Bribery, corruption, and extortion were rife amongst both Bolshevik officials and Red Guard men. Bolsheviks particularly oppressed Orthodox clergy and religion.

Czech soldier witnesses give evidences that near Khan Bolsheviks crucified father and sisters of man who served in national army; whole families of others in national army were shot. There is sufficient information to hand to be able to state that Bolsheviks' crimes in Ekaterinburg district are nothing in comparison with number and character of atrocities committed in Perm and district."

Mr. Alston to Earl Curzon.

(Telegraphic.) *Vladivostock, February* 13, 1919.
MR. T— has just arrived here from Ekaterinburg. When at Perm he says he lived in same hotel with Grand Duke Michael and Mr. Johnson, his secretary, who was a Russian. At 2 A.M. on or about the 16th June he saw four of Perm "militzia" or police take them off, and he is convinced that they were killed.

Previous reports of Bolshevik excesses at Perm are confirmed by Mr. T—, who says that usual method employed by them in the case of merchants was to arrest them, release them, rearrest them, bail them again—amount of bail to be paid increasing each time—and to shoot them in the end.

Acting Consul Bell to Earl Curzon.— (Received February 13.)

(Telegraphic.) *Helsingfors, February* 12, 1919.
I LEARN on good authority that Grand Dukes Paul Alexandrovitch, Dimitri Constantinovitch, Nickolai Michailovitch, Georges Michailovitch, who were all

confined in Petrograd in prison for preliminary investigation, were removed on 29th January, 1919, to
Peter and Paul fortress where, on the same day, without further investigations, they were killed by Red
Guards with revolver shots.

It is said that Princess Palej, widow of the late
Grand Duke Paul Alexandrovitch, escaped from
Petrograd after the murder of the Grand Duke.

Consul General Bagge to Earl Curzon.— (Received February 16.)

(Telegraphic.)   *Odessa, February* 13, 1919.
WIDESPREAD pillage by bands, murder of
landowners, even of peasants with few acres, has created very grave situation. Seed-grain is largely
lacking in consequence for spring sowing in
Ukraine. As these normally cover 70 per cent. of
whole area, if measures are not taken at once to
replace supply from Kuban and elsewhere, there will
be no crop and consequently terrible famine. This
state of things applies to peasants as well as large
landowners, the majority of whom have had to flee
to the coast towns.

The cardinal condition for saving Russia from
famine is maintenance of order in occupied territory
or South Russia. Thousands of peasant landowners,
when they have moral and some physical support,
will be able to cope with bands of robbers under
whatever names these may act. These peasants further
beg that property now existing in land be declared

inviolable until whole question shall be settled; without this assurance they do not care to risk expense of sowing for, perhaps, another to reap.

The question is very urgent, for work on land in the south begins in three to four weeks.

Sir C. Eliot to Earl Curzon.—(Received February 20.)

(Telegraphic.)   *Vladivostock, February* 19, 1919.

FOLLOWING from consul at Ekaterinburg:—

"Desertions from Red Army increasing, and peasants in Bolshevik Russia mutinying on mobilisation. Peasant insurrections occurred. Penza Government, also Ohansk, and Sizran districts. Mutinies of newly-mobilised troops took place at Tambof, Kursk, Kasan, Nijni Novgorod, and other places.

"According to Russian prisoner returning from Germany, insurrections against Bolsheviks took place between Vyatka and Glazof. Thirty Orthodox priests were massacred by Bolsheviks at Osa. Five hundred Russian officers returning from Germany shot at Menzelinsk."

Sir C. Eliot to Earl Curzon.—(Received February 23.)

(Telegraphic.)   *Vladivostock, February* 22, 1919.

FOLLOWING report of 71 Bolshevik victims received from consular officer at Ekaterinburg, dated 19th February:—

"Nos. 1 to 18 Ekaterinburg citizens (first 3

personally known to me) were imprisoned without any accusation being made against them, and at four in the morning of 29th June were taken (with another, making 19 altogether) to Ekaterinburg sewage dump, half mile from Ekaterinburg, and ordered to stand in line alongside of newly-dug ditch. Forty armed men in civil clothes, believed to be Communist militia, and giving impression of semi-intelligent people, opened fire, killing 18. The 19th, Mr. Chistoserdow, miraculously escaped in general confusion. I, together with other consuls at Ekaterinburg, protested to Bolsheviks against brutality, to which Bolsheviks replied, advising us to mind our own business, stating that they had shot these people to avenge death of their comrade, Malishef, killed at front, against Czechs.

"Nos. 19 and 20 are 2 of 12 labourers arrested for refusing to support Bolshevik Government, and on 12th July thrown alive into hole into which hot slag deposits from works at Verhisetski near Ekaterinburg. Bodies were identified by fellow labourers.

"Nos. 21 to 26 were taken as hostages and shot at Kamishlof on 20th July.

"Nos. 27 to 33, accused of plotting against Bolshevik Government, arrested 16th December at village of Troitsk, Perm Government. Taken 17th December to station Silva, Perm railway, and all decapitated by sword. Evidence shows that victims had their necks half cut through from behind, head of No. 29 only hanging on small piece of skin.

"Nos. 34 to 36, taken with 8 others beginning of

July from camp, where they were undergoing trench-digging service for Bolsheviks to spot near Oufalay, about 80 versts from Ekaterinburg, and murdered by Red Guards with guns and bayonets.

"Nos. 37 to 58, held in prison at Irbit as hostages, and 26th July murdered by gun-shot, those not killed outright being finished off by bayonet. These people were shot in small groups, and murder was conducted by sailors and carried out by Letts, all of whom were drunk. After murder, Bolsheviks continued to take ransom money from relatives of victims, from whom they concealed crime.

"No. 59 was shot at village Klevenkinski, Verhotury district, 6th August, being accused of agitation against Bolsheviks.

"No. 60, after being forced to dig his own grave, was shot by Bolsheviks at village Mercoushinski, Verhotury district, 13th July.

"No. 61 murdered middle of July at Kamenski works for allowing church bells to be sounded contrary to Bolshevik orders, body afterwards found with others in hole with head half cut off.

"No. 62 arrested without accusation, 8th July, at village Ooetski, Kamishlov district. Body afterwards found covered with straw and dung, beard torn from face with flesh, palms of hands cut out, and skin incised on forehead.

"No. 63 was killed after much torture (details not given), 27th July, at station Anthracite.

"No. 67 murdered, 13th August, near village of Mironoffski.

"No. 68 shot by Bolsheviks before his church at village of Korouffski, Kamishlov district, before eyes of villagers, his daughters and son, date not stated.

"Nos. 69 to 71, killed at Kaslingski works near Kishtim, 4th June, together with 27 other civilians. No. 70 had head smashed in, exposing brains. No. 71 had head smashed in, arms and legs broken, and two bayonet wounds.

"Dates in this telegram are 1918."

Sir C. Eliot to Earl Curzon.—(Received February 25.)

(Telegraphic.)   *Vladivostock, February* 24, 1919.
MY telegram of 22nd February.

Following from consul at Ekaterinburg:—

"Nos. 72 to 103 examined, 32 civilians incarcerated as hostages and taken away by Bolsheviks with 19 others at various dates between 9th July, 7th August, 27th July, all 51 having been declared outlaws. Official medical examination of 52 bodies (of which 32 examined, Nos. 72 to 103 and 20 not identified), found in several holes; 3 from Kamishlof revealed that all had been killed by bayonet, sword, and bullet wounds. Following cases being typical: No. 76 had 20 light bayonet wounds in back; No. 78 had 15 bayonet wounds in back, 3 in chest; No. 80, bayonet wounds in back, broken jaw and skull; No. 84, face smashed and wrist hacked; No. 89 had 2 fingers cut off and bayonet wounds; No. 90, both hands cut off at wrist, upper jaw hacked, mouth slit both sides, bayonet wound shoulder; No. 98, little finger off left hand and

4 fingers off right hand, head smashed; No. 99 had 12 bayonet wounds; No. 101 had 4 sword and 6 bayonet wounds.

"These victims are distinct from 66 Kamishlof hostage children shot by machine guns near Ekaterinburg beginning of July, names not obtainable."

Sir C. Eliot to Mr. Balfour.—(Received February 25.)

(Telegraphic.)   *Vladivostock, February* 24, 1919.
AN appeal to all democratic parties to unite against Bolsheviks has been published by the Omsk Government. Reasons given are as follow:—

1. Dictatorship of one class was claimed by Bolsheviks, and people of other classes were placed outside the law and starved.

2. Bolsheviks have deprived educated classes of their votes, as they do not admit universal suffrage.

3. Bureaucracy has been set up in place of municipal and village government, which has been abolished.

4. Political organisations have replaced Law Courts.

General Knox to War Office.

(Telegraphic.)   *Vladivostock, March* 2, 1919.
FOLLOWING received from Omsk, 26th February:—

"Position of railway transport critical. Owing to absence of metals, coal, and spare parts, workshops on railways have ceased work. Passenger traffic continues only on Nikolaevski Railway, only military and food trains running on other railways.

"Money being printed on colossal scale, 14,000 workmen employed in Petrograd and Pensa day and night. 300 million notes of different valuations are said to be daily turned out. Peasants very hostile to Soviet's action, and riots resulted in many quarters.

"Discipline growing stricter in army. Return of shoulder straps and saluting being considered.

"In near future the Bolsheviks intend closing all churches. Three priests were recently drowned by Reds in Osa."

General Knox to War Office.

Vladivostock, March 4, 1919.

AN interview with an officer has appeared in a Vladivostock paper which gives an idea of the ruin that has befallen Moscow. He had escaped through the lines, and says that executions and arrests, to say nothing of hunger and cold and robbery in all its forms, are part of the daily life of the city. The streets are filthy and torn up, houses are shell-shattered and gutted by fire. Pocket-picking has become fashionable, and is looked on as a harmless eccentricity. Officers are put on to the most menial forms of work, such as street cleaning, loading bricks at railway stations, and a colonel is now a night watchman. Whilst Kuksh was in Bolshevik occupation women from 16 to 50 were mobilised for work, and to "satisfy the needs of the pride and flower of the revolution." At Goroblagodatsky the Red Army threw forty-four bodies down a well. They were discovered later, and amongst them were found the bodies of a priest, some monks, and a young girl. At Blagoveschensk officers and soldiers from Torbolof's detachment were found with gramophone needles thrust under their finger nails, their eyes torn out, the marks of nails on their shoulders where shoulder straps had been worn. Their bodies had become like frozen statues, and were hideous to look upon. These men had been killed by Bolsheviks at Metzanovaya and taken thence to Blagoveschensk.

Following is text of document belonging to a Red Commissar captured at front and quoted in local press:—

"Herewith I certify that the bearer, comrade Evdomikof, is allowed the right of acquiring a girl for himself and no one may oppose this in any way, he is invested with full power which I certify."

Sir C. Eliot to Earl Curzon.—(Received March 7.)

(Telegraphic.)   *Vladivostock, March* 5, 1919.

FOLLOWING from consul at Ekaterinburg, 3rd March:—

"Following is summary of Bolshevik investigation at Perm. Commencing from February 1918 factories were managed by Labour Committees amongst whom criminals were to be found; incapacity of these committees and general demoralisation of labouring class brought about complete standstill of production and rise in prices from which whole population suffers.

"Bolsheviks completely disorganised school establishments by appointing teachers by system of voting in which students and domestic employees of schools took part. First-year law students appointed by Bolsheviks replaced magistrates in Law Courts.

"Bolshevik policy was characterised by persecution of all classes of population suspected of ill-feeling towards them, especially well-to-do class and peasants.

"In spite of confiscation of their property well-to-do class were forced to pay huge contributions and many of them were arrested as hostages on most futile pretexts, without any accusations being made against them and frequently by caprice or personal spite of some Bolshevist commissary.

"Those who were not shot were incarcerated under disgraceful conditions where they were kept under perpetual dread of being murdered. During arrest of these people their houses were pillaged.

"In villages 'poor committees' were organised, representatives of which were supposed to be elected by peasants; elections were, however, discarded tacitly by Bolsheviks, who appoint people almost exclusively of criminal classes. Contributions, requisitions, and other tyrannies were imposed by Bolsheviks on peasants possessing land or other property, which resulted in insurrections in villages suppressed by Bolsheviks by pillage, devastations, and massacres on large scale, notably at Sepytchyi and Pystor in Ohansk district, August 1918. Labourers opposing Bolsheviks were treated in same manner as peasants. One hundred labourers were shot at Motovilyky near Perm, December 1918, for protesting against Bolshevik conduct. Peasants particularly suffered when Red Army retreated, Bolsheviks taking with them cereals, horses, and cattle available, and destroying all agricultural and other instruments they were not able to take with them. Bolshevik persecution of anti-Bolshevik elements reached height of its fury after attempt on Lenin's life, although even previously it had developed into a reign of terror.

"Commissaries consisted of unintellectual labourers from 20 to 30 years' old who condemned people to death without making any accusation against them, frequently personally taking part in murder of their victims.

"Russian authorities have only just commenced investigation of Bolshevik crimes, and therefore it is difficult to obtain precise data as to number of persons killed, although, as far as we can judge, it runs into several thousands in Perm Government. Victims were usually shot, but frequently drowned or killed by sword. Murders of groups of 30, 40, and 60 have taken place, for example at Perm and Kungur.

"Murders were frequently preceded by tortures and acts of cruelty. Labourers at Omsk, before being shot, were flogged and beaten with butts of rifles and pieces of iron in order to extract evidence. Victims were frequently forced to dig their own graves. Sometimes executioners placed them facing wall and fired several revolver shots from behind them, near their ears, killing them after considerable interval;

persons who survived this gave evidence.

"Girls, aged women, and women *enceintes* were amongst victims. Case of Miss Bakouyeva is an example. December, 1918, this lady (19 years old) was accused of espionage, and tortured by being slowly pierced thirteen times in same wound by bayonet. She was afterwards found by peasants still alive; is now nearly cured, and has herself related her sufferings to us.

"Bolshevists vented violent hatred on church and clergy, pillaged monasteries (such as Bielogorod and Bielogorski), turned churches into meeting places and work-shops, persecuted and murdered priests and monks; of 300 priests in liberated parts of Perm diocese, 46 were killed by Bolshevists."

Sir C. Eliot to Earl Curzon.—(Received March 26.)

(Telegraphic.) *Vladivostock, March* 21, 1919. FOLLOWING from consul at Ekaterinburg, 20th March:—

"Have now completed our report on Bolsheviks. Enclosures comprise Russian consul's unbiased evidence of nearly 100 witnesses, 20 photographs of atrocities committed by Bolsheviks and other documentary evidence obtained from Russian authorities.

"Persons of all classes, especially peasants, continue to come to this consulate, giving evidence of murder of their relatives and other outrages that Bolsheviks in their fury have wrought, but, owing to necessity of limiting work in order to complete report, have been obliged to curtail taking further evidence.

"Details given in my recent telegrams may be taken as characteristic of manner Bolsheviks murdered innocent citizens; and, therefore, for reasons above mentioned, unless I hear from you to contrary, shall desist from sending you further names. From reports received, murder and pillage committed by Bolsheviks during their retreat from this front assumed most terrible proportions."

Extract from a Report by a British Chaplain.
WITH the oncoming of the Austro-German armies
into South Russia last spring, my experiences of
Bolshevism entered on a new phase. Previously I had
for many months lived in the terrorised city of
Odessa, where the cowed and despoiled population
had been bullied into abject submission to a brutal
and despotic Bolshevik tyranny. The city had been
drenched with blood; murders and outrages in the
streets as well as houses were of daily, even hourly
occurrence; trade was paralysed, shops looted, the

bourgeoisie arrested, tortured, and done to death by hundreds under circumstances of fiendish cruelty. The Allied consuls had left, and the majority of the foreigners, when a general massacre of the educated population was arranged to commence with the extermination of 108 families. This last brutality was averted by the arrival of the armies of the Central Powers.

Undoubtedly the rapidly accumulating horrors were deliberately incited by the secret German Bolshevik agents in order that the advancing Austrian armies might not be met as foes but welcomed as deliverers coming to save the people from a tyranny more brutal than anything Russia had previously known. The scheme was entirely successful; the Austrian troops were received as saviours.

The intrigue was cleverly managed. Nothing had been left to chance. All possibility of effective armed opposition had been rendered impossible by the enormous massacres of Russian officers previously systematically incited by the German propagandists. The march into the Southern Ukraine was another stage in a Vienna intrigue, which has been moving forward for the last forty years: the design for expansion to the East and access to the Black Sea.

Within three days of the arrival of the Austrian army in Odessa, the soldiers were sent into the city with orders to fraternise with the inhabitants, to conduct themselves with marked courtesy and self-restraint, and to meet all friendly advances with conciliatory affability.

The Russian Bolshevik troops fled at the approach of the Austrians. The Black Sea fleet left the morning Odessa was surrendered. Some of the ships were so heavily laden with plunder they could scarcely make way. A large proportion of the worst Bolshevik criminals of the district, together with the more notorious bands of assassins and highwaymen, escaped with the fleet. Two of the crews, having murdered their officers some time before, were unable to navigate their vessels until help was sent from other ships. The Bolshevik flagship took on board the entire company from the two largest houses of ill-fame in the city together with their private orchestra. For three days before the Austrians marched into Odessa the Bolsheviks had divers at work from the Imperial yacht "Almas" and the cruiser "Sinope" dragging the harbour for the weighted bodies of the murdered officers, of whom about 400 had been done to death, the majority after torture with boiling steam followed by exposure to currents of freezing air. Others were burnt alive, bound to planks which were slowly pushed into the furnaces a few inches at a time. In this way perished General Chourmakof and many others of my acquaintance. The bodies now recovered from the water were destroyed in the ships' furnaces that no evidence might remain to be brought before the Austro-Germans. Later, a member of the Austrian Staff told me they had been supplied with a list of names of over 400 murdered officers from the Odessa district.

January, 1919.

———

M. M— to Earl Curzon.—(Received February 8.)

Moscow, January 12, 1919.

I HAVE the honour to report that the food question in Moscow is growing more and more acute with every day. Nominally the population of this city has to obtain its food by the card system, cards of three categories having been introduced and the quantity of food available distributed in the following proportions:—

Category 1. Those working manual work   4
     "   2. Those working intellectual ...   3
     "   3. Those having no employment   2

The difficulty, however, is that no food, except black bread, is available for distribution, and the quantity of bread distributed at present, namely, $\frac{1}{2}$–pound for the first category, $\frac{3}{8}$–pound for the second, and $\frac{1}{4}$–pound for the third, is completely insufficient to keep one alive. Other food-stuffs must be obtained from speculators at exorbitant prices, the seller as well as the purchaser running the risk of a heavy fine or imprisonment if denounced, as traffic in food-stuffs is strictly forbidden.

Thousands of men and women are going daily to distant country places with the object of purchasing and bringing into town some provisions, thus disarranging the regular railway traffic.

It is, however, not an easy matter to bring provisions into Moscow, as cordons of soldiers are searching passengers' luggage at country stations, and will take away, at their discretion, anything they think superfluous.

Lord Kilmarnock to Earl Curzon.—(Received February 24.)

My Lord,   *Copenhagen, February* 17, 1919.
I HAVE the honour to transmit, herewith, translations of two further reports on the atrocities committed by the Bolsheviks in the Baltic Provinces which have been furnished me by the Esthonian Provisional Government here.

I also enclose seven photographs of the victims of the massacres by the Bolsheviks at Wesenberg and Dorpat from the same source.

> I have, &c.
> KILMARNOCK.

Enclosure
BOLSHEVIK ATROCITIES IN ESTHONIA.

Further Supplementary Reports.
ON the 25th December the Bolsheviks shot the steward, Karu, the foreman, and the housekeeper, Sitau, of the Kiltsi estate. Before death, the victims were cruelly tortured. Besides these, the author, Woldemar Rosenstrauch, and three other persons were shot.

According to the report from the leader of an attacking squadron, Lieutenant Jakobsen, the Bolsheviks murdered two brothers, Hendrik and Hans Kokamal, of Piksaare, on the 26th January. They crushed the head of the former by two blows of an axe, and shot the latter. Besides this, they robbed the victims of their clothes and boots and tore their linen, which, being bloodstained, was useless to them.

In Sagnitz, in the Walk district, the head forester, Hesse, and the book-keeper, Wichmann, were shot by the Bolsheviks. As well as the graves of these two victims, seven more were discovered at the same place.

The Blood-Bath in Walk.
BOLSHEVISM raged more in Walk than anywhere else, as the Bolsheviks remained longest in power

there. The number of persons murdered by them is great, but not definitely known. At all events they are estimated at from 350 to 450. Besides, 600 to 700 persons were carried off by the Bolsheviks. From the report of the inhabitants of the district, these unfortunates were murdered on the way.

The murders were committed in the same manner as elsewhere. The unfortunates, who belonged to different classes of society, were arrested on all sorts of pretexts, kept prisoners a few days, and then, in groups of twenty to thirty, led out of the town to the place of execution, where graves were already prepared for them. Every night, twenty to thirty persons were executed without examination or trial. Before being shot, the victims were tortured in every possible way. All the bodies bear marks of many bayonet thrusts as well as gun wounds. The skulls are shattered and the bones broken. Even after death, when the bodies were stiff, the Bolsheviks hacked off the arms and legs and broke the bones of their victims.

The Bolsheviks have instilled such terror into the hearts of the local inhabitants, that they dare not even talk of the Bolsheviks' deeds, and therefore it is difficult to obtain a true report of all their atrocities in Walk.

An Esthonian soldier of cavalry was taken prisoner by the Bolsheviks and was to be executed in Walk along with many others. The Bolshevik bullets, which killed so many of his comrades, did not hit him, and he succeeded after the murder to escape from the common burial-place. He describes one of those terrible blood-baths in the following manner:—

"They took our caps, coats, and cloaks. Thirty-five armed Bolsheviks surrounded us in order to prevent any attempt at escape. Our hands were bound behind our backs. Besides this, we were fastened in couples, and then each pair joined by a long rope, so that we marched all attached to the one rope. Thus we were led to death. As I protested against this barbaric treatment, the Bolshevik officer struck me twice on the head with a riding-whip and said, 'Shooting is too good for you, your eyes ought to be put out before death.' At the word of command, the Bolsheviks fired a volley. The bound group fell to earth. I also was pulled down by the others, though I had not been hit. The Bolsheviks fired four rounds on the fallen. Fortunately, I again was missed. Then the execution-ers fell upon us like wild animals to rob us. Anyone who still moved was finally killed by bayonets or blows from the butt-ends of rifles. I kept as still as possible. One of the Bolsheviks took my boots. Another looked at my stockings. 'Good stockings,' he murmured, and pulled them off."

It is reported from Werro:—

The rapidity with which the Esthonian troops occupied Werro saved the lives of more than 200 people. There were 183 persons in prison, for whom a similar fate was intended as befell those in Dorpat on the 14th January. The lists were already made out. But the Red Guard took flight at the approach of the

Esthonian troops. Only the warders remained behind, and they opened the prison doors. Altogether some 100 people were to have been shot in Werro near the Russian cemetery, Kaseritzschen lake, and Kirrumpäh redoubt. On the arrival of the rescuers many of the graves were not yet filled in, and a number of bodies lay exposed in the snow. Several women were also shot, and especially ghastly was the murder of Frl. Irmgard Kupffer. The following are the names of people who are known to have been murdered in Werro:— Barber Kuns, Solicitor R. Pihlak, House-owners Kond and Wierland, Forester Matson from Erastwere, Pastor Sommer, and Hr. Wreemann. The names of most of the victims are unknown, for the greater number did not belong to Werro, but had been carried off there from the neighbouring villages and shot. The Bolsheviks also kept secret the number and names of their victims.

It has already been mentioned that, according to the Bolshevik newspaper "Tööline," a number of counter-revolutionaries were murdered in Werro on the 14th January. Now information is brought by Merchant P. , of Pölwa, who was led to death with the above-mentioned victims, but who escaped the massacre. He reports the following: "The twenty-four men who were condemned to death were led to a lake. There they were ordered to undress and to run home. The victims obeyed, but scarcely had they turned their backs when the Bolsheviks fired a volley at them. P. saved himself by throwing himself on the ground in good time. The Bolsheviks, thinking he was dead like the others, went off. Then P. got up and went away. Three or four victims saved themselves in this way, whilst the others were fatally shot by the Bolsheviks."

A few days after the retreat from Dorpat the Bolsheviks shot three people, namely, Täkk, Waltin, and Antzow.

According to later news, the following people were shot by the Bolsheviks: Steward Hansen of the Arral estate near Odenpäh, with his son, and Herr Seen, the owner of Saarjerw, in Pölwe.

It is reported from Walk that, among others, the Bolsheviks shot Police Inspector Koch, and the former Ensign Rudolf. They carried away the following persons: Pastors Wühuer, Uns, Jänes, Michelson, Priests Protopopow, Sirnis, and Merchant Wassili.

Summary of a Report on the Internal Situation in Russia.

THE following is a summary of a report on the internal situation in Russia which has been received from Mr. K—, a member of the British Printers' Trade Union, who left Petrograd on the 9th January, 1919. Mr. K— was also a member of the Russian Printers' Trade Union; he travelled extensively in Russia and was received everywhere as a working man. He had, therefore, an exceptional opportunity of studying the conditions in Soviet Russia. Reports have been received from various sources of the growing opposition to Bolshevik rule among a certain section of the Russian population, and Mr. K—'s account tends to confirm these reports:—

(i.) *Conditions in the towns.*—Since the beginning of November, 1918, there has been an increasingly strong feeling against the Bolsheviks among the intelligent portions of the working classes of Petrograd, Moscow, and other centres. In the early days of their power the Bolsheviks were enthusiastically supported by the working classes in the towns, but latterly the more enlightened have become convinced of the failure of the Bolsheviks' experiments at social reform. They have, however, nominally remained Bolsheviks, as there is no other alternative, since the Bolsheviks control the food supplies and hold all the arms in the country. Mr. K—, in support of the foregoing, quotes views expressed to him by members of various factory staffs, and he cites cases of strikes in large factories, such as the Putilov, Obukhovski, Treugolnik, of which confirmation has been received from other sources. All factories are controlled by the Soviet of People's Economy. The Commissars are inexperienced, and great difficulty is experienced in obtaining good workmen, with the result that the output of the factories has greatly decreased, in some cases to 10 per cent of the original output.

Note.—Further confirmation of the reported opposition of a section of the working population to Bolshevik rule is found in a recent Bolshevik wireless message, which states that 60,000 workmen are on strike in Petrograd, demanding an end to fratricidal war and the institution of free trade.

(ii.) *Conditions in the countryside.*—A similar change has occurred in the attitude of the better-class peasants. At first Bolshevik innovations were welcomed in the countryside, where, also, feeling was bitter against the English, who were accused of the desire to exploit Russia for their benefit. This attitude, however, underwent a change when the Poverty Committees were instituted. These committees were composed of the worst elements of the villages reinforced by Bolsheviks from the towns, with the result that village life became intolerable. Respectable peasants, to remedy this state of affairs, decided to join these committees with a view to exercising their influence upon them, and in many cases were successful. This led to a change in the constitution of the committees, and the Soviet authorities are now endeavouring to regain their former control in this respect. At the same time the peasants' attitude of hostility towards the English disappeared, and the wish was expressed in many quarters that the latter would come and deliver Russia from Bolshevik rule.

(iii.) *Religious revival.*—Another important factor in

the situation has been a strong revival of religious feeling in the towns and countryside; the result, apparently, of the revulsion caused by the wholesale persecution and murder of priests by the Bolsheviks. The change of attitude in this respect is manifest by the great increase in church attendance, which in the early days of Bolshevik rule was chiefly confined to women, and by the increasing boldness of the priests in denouncing the Bolsheviks. It is noteworthy, in the latter respect, that the priests are acting with increasing impunity—a fact which appears to indicate that the Bolsheviks are afraid of antagonising public opinion over this question.

Anti-Bolshevik conspiracy.—In the above connection, and as further evidence of the growing opposition, in the interior, to the Bolsheviks, it is of interest to note that, according to the Bolshevik wireless news of the 14th February, an anti-Bolshevik conspiracy on the part of Left Social Revolutionaries has been discovered. The headquarters of the conspiracy were at Moscow. The leaders, it is stated, which include Mme. Spiridonova, Steinberg, Trutovsky, Protapovitch, and Rozenblum, have been arrested, and the movement has apparently been completely forestalled. It is stated that documentary evidence shows that the object of these Left Social Revolutionaries was to overthrow the Soviet Government and to establish an all-Russian Government. As a preliminary step, terroristic acts were to be carried out against Soviet leaders; these, however, were to be carried out independently by local organisations with a view to avoid compromising the whole movement. Steps had been taken to institute anti-Bolshevik propaganda in the army and among the peasants, who were to be incited to rise. The chief activities of this organisation had apparently been directed towards White Russia, where, in the "Nash Put" (the Vilna organ of the Left Social Revolutionaries), an anti-Bolshevik agitation had already commenced. In White Russia it was apparently the aim of this organisation to seize power on the evacuation of the German forces.

Rev. B. S. Lombard to Earl Curzon.

Officers' Quarters, 8, Rothsay Gardens, Bedford.
My Lord,   *March* 23, 1919.
I BEG to forward to your Lordship the following details with reference to Bolshevism in Russia:—

I have been for ten years in Russia, and have been in Petrograd through the whole of the revolution.

I spent six weeks in the Fortress of Peter and Paul, acted as chaplain to His Majesty's submarines in the Baltic for four years, and was in contact with the 9th (Russian) Army in Roumania during the autumn of 1917 whilst visiting British Missions and hospitals, and had ample opportunity of studying Bolshevik methods.

It originated in German propaganda, and was, and is, being carried out by international Jews.

The Germans initiated disturbances in order to reduce Russia to chaos. They printed masses of paper money to finance their schemes, the notes of which I possess specimens can be easily recognised by a special mark.

Their Tenets.
Radically to destroy all ideas of patriotism and nationality by preaching the doctrine of internationalism which proved successful amongst the uncultured masses of the labouring classes.

To obstruct by every means the creation of military power by preaching the ideas of peace, and to foster the abolition of military discipline.

To keep the masses under the hypnosis of false Socialistic literature.

To buy up all nationalised banks and to open up everywhere branches of German Government banks under the names and titles of firms that would conceal their actual standing.

To endeavour to empoverish and temporally to weaken the peasant classes, to bring about national calamities such as epidemics (the outbreak of cholera last summer was traced to this source), the wholesale burning down of villages and settlements.

To preach the doctrine of the Socialistic form of managing enterprises amongst the working classes, to encourage their efforts to seize such enterprises and then by means of bankruptcies to get them into German hands.

To preach the idea of a six to eight hours' working day with higher wages.

To crush all competition set on foot against them. All attempts of the intellectuals or other groups to undertake any kind of independent action, or to develop any industries to be unmercifully checked, and in doing this to stop at nothing.

Russia to be inundated by commission agents and other German representatives, and a close network of agencies and offices should be created for the purpose of spreading amongst the masses such views and teachings as may at any given time be dictated from Berlin.

The Results.

All business became paralysed, shops were closed, Jews became possessors of most of the business houses, and horrible scenes of starvation became common in the country districts. The peasants put their children to death rather than see them starve. In a village on the Dvina, not far from Schlusselberg, a mother hanged three of her children.

I was conducting a funeral in a mortuary of a lunatic asylum at Oudelnaia, near Petrograd, and saw the bodies of a mother and her five children whose throats had been cut by the father because he could not see them suffer.

When I left Russia last October the nationalisation of women was regarded as an accomplished fact, though I cannot prove that (with the exception of at Saratoff) there was any actual proclamation issued.

The cruelty of the soldiers is unspeakable. The father of one of the Russian clerks in the Vauxhall Motor Works was bound and laid on a railway line and cut to pieces by a locomotive on suspicion of having set fire to some of his own property. In August last two bargeloads of Russian officers were sunk and their bodies washed up on the property of a friend of mine in the Gulf of Finland, many lashed together in twos and threes with barbed wire.

While we were in prison a Red Guard was sent from the central police station (Gorokovaya 2) in charge of five prisoners to the fortress. One of them, an old officer, was unable to walk, the guard shot him and left his body on the Troytsky Bridge. The murderer was reprimanded and imprisoned in a cell near ours. The treatment of priests was brutal beyond everything. Eight of them were incarcerated in a cell in our corridor. Some of us saw an aged man knocked down twice one morning for apparently no reason whatever, and they were employed to perform the most degrading work and made to clean out the filthy prison hospital. Recently, life in Petrograd has become a veritable nightmare.

In the early days of 1917 the Russians gloried in a bloodless revolution, now they simply glut themselves with killing for the most trivial offences. In a market on the opposite side of the river to my house, a poor woman with a starving family filched a small piece of meat from a stall; without any hesitation the Red Guard surrounded her and placing her against a wall shot her dead.

The rank and file of the Red Army is full of men who are heartily sick of the present régime, and would gladly join any really strong force sent to the relief of the country. But unless the force were considerable, they would hesitate.

But I imagine that the food question is the key to the situation, the Red Armies must be at a low ebb for provisions, and by getting stores to Helsingfors they might be treated with.

I am, &c.

BOUSFIELD S. LOMBARD,

Chaplain to the Forces.

Interviews with returned British subjects.

MR. A— left Petrograd in November. He stated that production was practically at a standstill, and in the most favourable cases has decreased 50 per cent. The factories are run by Committees. A Committee composed of Mensheviks produces a fair amount of work, but a Committee of Bolsheviks gives a wholly unsatisfactory output. The Committees were formerly elective, but the Bolsheviks now co-opt their own members without consulting the workpeople, and members who do not agree with the Bolsheviks are voted off. The Committees are in fact entirely political, and there is a great increase of bureaucracy.

Discipline is bad, and the men are frequently one or one and a half hours late. The responsible members of the Committee do not understand the needs of the mill, and the Bolsheviks object to paying technical men.

In May 1918 an attempt of the Committee to form their own organisation was rigorously suppressed.

Mr. B—, who has lived in Russia all his life, left Moscow on the 8th February and was interviewed at the Foreign Office on his arrival, and supplied the following information:—

Food Conditions
The food conditions are getting worse and worse every day, and it is now practically impossible to obtain enough to eat. People are dying of starvation everywhere. A few months ago it was possible for the townspeople to buy food from the peasants down in the villages, but they are unable to do this now, as the peasants will not take money for any food that they may have to sell. Everything is done by exchange. Money is no use to the peasants, but clothes and instruments are valuable, so the exchange system is used everywhere.

The following are the most recent prices of food:—

Moscow—	Roubles.
1 lb. of bread	16
1 ,, potatoes	6

1 lb. butter		100–120
1 „ lard		85–90
1 „ oil (used instead of butter)		45–55
1 pint of milk		12
1 lb. of meat		30–35
1 „ pork		65–75
1 „ horse meat		15–17
1 „ dog's meat		5–7
1 cat is sold for		6

There are three food categories in Moscow now instead of four, but even the "category" people cannot get all the food they are entitled to receive. Certainly the 1st category ought to receive $\frac{1}{2}$-lb. bread a day, the 2nd, $\frac{3}{8}$-lb., and the 3rd, $\frac{1}{8}$-lb.; also about $\frac{1}{2}$-lb. to 1-lb. of fish a month, which was usually not fit for consumption; $1\frac{1}{4}$ to $1\frac{1}{2}$ lb. of oil a month (butter substitute); and about $\frac{1}{2}$-lb. soap a month. The above is all that could be obtained even by category people. No fats of any description were obtainable. Mr. B— himself sold a lb. of soap for 35 roubles.

In spite of the appalling conditions prevailing everywhere, the Kremlin is well supplied with all kinds of food. A servant of the house where Mr. B— stayed had a brother in the Kremlin, and he told her that there was an abundance of ham, white bread, butter, sausages, &c.

Disease

Typhus is rampant everywhere, and is getting worse every day. There is also a lot of typhoid fever about; but, worse than this, glanders is now spreading among the people. The Bolsheviks are afraid of this terrible disease spreading far and wide, so they simply shoot any person suffering from this complaint. There are no medicines there by which they can attempt to cure the people, and there is of course a great shortage of doctors. Mr. B— thinks that there are more cases of glanders in Moscow than anywhere else.

Fuel Shortage
The people are suffering intensely from the cold as there is practically no wood available. Only $3\frac{1}{2}$ feet of wood is allowed a month for one flat, and even this the people have to fetch themselves from the railway stations. The price of wood in the Nijni Novgorod is 200 roubles a fathom (official price); if bought from outside (in the markets, &c.) it is about 500 roubles. The average heat of a room is only 43° to 45° Fahrenheit. The fuel question is much worse in Petrograd than it is in Moscow. The reason for this is that most of the Petrograd houses have central heating, and when the pipes get out of order (as they invariably do) there is no possibility of ever having them mended.

Factories and Workmen
All the workmen are anti-Bolshevik in reality, though many of them have to work under the Bolsheviks in order to live. Mr. B— gave 5 to 10 per cent. as his estimate of the number of Bolsheviks out of the whole population of Russia.

The Bolsheviks pay the workmen very well, but

as the cost of living has increased so tremendously their wages are not nearly high enough to enable them to live comfortably, even were the food obtainable. Roughly speaking, the workmen get fifteen to twenty times as much as they used to, and the cost of living has gone up to anything between 300 and 1000 times as much as it was before the Revolution.

The Bolsheviks employ very high-handed methods with the factories. If the workmen strike, the factory is closed, the leaders are generally arrested, and sometimes they are even shot. At the Sokolnitski works (repairing trams, &c.) in Moscow, the workmen men went on strike because the Bolsheviks said they were not turning out the proper amount of work. As a result of this the factory was simply closed down and the following notice was put in the paper: "In consequence of the falling off of production in the Sokolnitski works, it was closed down by order of the Government." All this proves that the Workmen's Committees have no real power, as the Bolsheviks just do what they like without even consulting the Committees.

At S——, where Mr. B—— was working, the Bolsheviks wanted to inaugurate a demonstration on the 25th October, 1918. In order to get the men to attend the demonstration meeting the Bolsheviks promised a free dinner to all who went, and looked upon those who refused as saboteurs. This, in the end, practically amounted to forcing the men to join the demonstration.

There are not many factories working in Russia now; most of them have had to close down on account of the fuel shortage. The few factories that remain only work about three days a week, but the workmen are paid full wages. Often a factory has to be closed for weeks at a time, owing to lack of fuel and raw material; during this time the workmen are paid half wages.

Political Questions

The people have no interest at all in politics, the only topic of conversation being food. Everyone would welcome Allied intervention; in fact, anything would be preferable to the Bolshevik régime. Mr. B— does not think that many troops would be required, as the Red Army is of small account, and directly they got there it would go to pieces. In fact, the only reason why the officers stay in the army is because the Bolsheviks threaten to shoot their wives, mothers, or sisters if they desert. Mr. B— has spoken to officers, the addresses of whose families had been taken down by the Bolsheviks for this reason.

In Moscow the Menshevik paper, "Vperyod," was allowed to reappear for a few days, but it was soon suppressed. It then appeared later under the name of "Vsegda Vperyod" ("Always Forward"). The "Izvestiya" still attacks the Mensheviks, in spite of the so-called agreement which the Bolsheviks have made so much use of for propaganda abroad.

General Conditions

To take a cab to the station costs 120 roubles, and even at this price it is very difficult to obtain a cab at all.

The "terror" is not so bad as it used to be, but this is merely because the people's spirit is quite broken, and they do not dare to offer opposition.

Education

Students of the high schools do not pay any fees, and any boy or girl of 16 years of age is allowed to enter the universities without showing any certificates, so that if a boy is unable to read or write he can still go to the university. This offer of education does not appeal to the working-class very much, and it is mostly the *intelligentsia* who take advantage of this opportunity.

In spite of the Bolsheviks' so-called efforts to promote education, nothing is being accomplished, and things are going from bad to worse. They have instituted workmen's clubs where the workmen can go and listen to lectures, &c., but the only reason why any men attend is because a cup of tea and a slice of bread is usually supplied sometime during the lecture. In the same way, the only reason why children go to school is to get the breakfast that is given there.

Journey to England

Mr. B— came to England with twelve other Englishmen, and they had to go through some very trying ordeals before getting out of Russia. They were packed in two cattle trucks, and it took them sixty-eight hours instead of twelve to get from Moscow to Petrograd. They had to do their own stoking and find their own fuel, &c., and they also had to feed the engine driver.

During the journey one Bolshevik woman told Mr. B— that all the railway men ought to be shot as they were hostile to the Bolsheviks.

Between the big stations only two trains run a day: one in the morning and one at night. The whole question of transport is exceedingly bad.

Mr. C—, formerly with T— and Co., and then with Moscow branch of Anglo-Russian Commission, left Russia on the 21st January.

Factories and Workmen

All factories nationalised; only about half of them working. Men all anti-Bolshevik. Very discontented with conditions of life, and with the working of the factories. Conditions getting worse and worse every day. Great many of the men have gone to the country, as it is practically impossible to live in the towns.

Mr. C—, after leaving Anglo-Russian Commission, went to the factory where he used to work to seek employment, but the factory had been nationalised and they refused to employ him, saying he was a counter-revolutionary (because an Englishman).

At one time Mr. C— lived near cotton mill belonging to L—. All the workmen there are against the Bolsheviks and very discontented, but they have to go on working for the Bolsheviks in order to live. Factory works about three days a week on a 6-hour day. Often have to stop work for a week or two because there is no fuel or no cotton left; have to wait until new supply comes in. Very often about ten factories combine and work under a common directorship: this is done in order that one factory may exchange with another whatever is wanted. If one of these factories is closed down, the village members of the other factories are discharged, and the men from the old factory employed in their places.

In Petrograd more attempts to strike than in Moscow; this is because in Moscow the workmen are more under the power of the Government, and they do not dare to strike. Even if they did there is nothing to gain by it, for the Government would simply stop their wages, discharge a good many, and probably cancel their bread cards.

Moscow

In Moscow all shops are closed, with the exception of Soviet shops. All hotels taken up long ago by Red Guard detachments, &c. Nothing can be purchased from the shops without a ticket or order, and this ticket can only be obtained by a Soviet worker, and even he has to go from one place to another before the ticket is legal. First he has to get a ticket from his factory, then he has to go to his trade union, and so on, before he is entitled to buy anything. An ordinary man is unable to purchase anything.

Fur coats, which had been requisitioned by the Soviet, were sold at the Soviet shops for, say, two, three or four hundred roubles. The next day the same fur coats were sold down in the thieves' market for about 7,000 roubles.

Mr. C— sold a very old suit (privately, as public selling is forbidden), for which he got 600 roubles.

Services are not held in the church because there is no fuel to heat the building. As there are only a few people left to attend services, the priest holds them in his own house.

When Red Guards are sent from Moscow to the front there is often a row at the station, and guns are taken from them. When they eventually arrive at front, often only half of original number present, the rest having escaped. The Red Guards are quite content to receive good pay, &c., but they are not anxious to fight.

Theatres still running very well. Actors are greatly privileged, being placed in first category, &c.

Bookshops distribute literature free in the villages, and in Moscow it is sold very cheap. No tickets required for books.

Between 50 and 100 Englishmen left in Moscow.

Mr. D—, who has been in Russia for three or four years, left Moscow on the 21st January.

Mr. D— was giving private lessons all the time he was in Russia, but during the last month or so he went as a teacher of French to one of the lower grade schools in Moscow. The reason for this was that he found it practically impossible to live on the fourth category, and by going to a school he was transferred to the third category.

Discipline in the school very bad indeed. The only reason why children or teachers went to school at all was in order to get the food supplied there.

Food conditions were very bad indeed. No provision shops open in Moscow. The people are all anti-Bolshevik at heart, but they have to work for the Bolsheviks in order to live.

Typhus is rampant, and many people are suffering from skin diseases (Mr. D— himself experienced this) caused from the want of fats.

Only a few trams and trains running, and the former often have to stop for a day or two on account of disputes and strikes.

The fuel question is very serious, and it is becoming more and more acute every day. Some friends of Mr. D— had no means of cooking the little food they had, as they had no benzine, no kerosene, and no wood. People often have to cut up chairs, tables, &c., for firewood.

Moscow is a dead city. Very few trams running, many shops boarded up, all shop-signs removed. The whole place looks deserted. The houses are all in bad condition, &c. But, in Mr. D—'s opinion, the streets of Moscow are much safer now than they were a year ago. There is no street robbery, and the only danger now is being arrested in the street.

Mr. D— thinks there are still about sixty or seventy English people left in Moscow.

Bolshevik literature impresses the people to some extent, but they don't *want* to believe it.

The people are waiting and hoping for some sort

of intervention from England. The present position is intolerable, and practically anything would be preferable to the Bolshevik rule.

Mr. E——, secretary of a bank, left Russia on the 24th January. He supplied the following information:—

It is impossible to live in Petrograd, as the prices are outrageous. There are only two categories now, the 1st and 2nd. The 1st category consists of people working in the different Bolshevik works and organisations; physical workers, their wives, and their children (up to 12 years of age). The 2nd category consists of all those who either support themselves by their own labour (either mental or physical), and do not live by interest on accrued capital, or who do not use the fruits of other people's labour. The Red Guards are always considered first, and practically form a category of their own, which is higher than either the 1st or 2nd. Officially, the 1st category ought to receive 1-lb. of bread a day, and the 2nd $\frac{1}{4}$-lb., but in reality the amount varies from day to day, according to the supplies. The 3rd and 4th categories have been done away with altogether; consequently, there are a great many people who are in no category at all. The Bolsheviks published statistics showing that the 4th category was not necessary, as there were so few members. This proves that the 4th category people have either been exterminated or have been forced to work under the Bolsheviks in order to live. Three months ago, a decree was issued saying that all those about to enter the 1st category must produce a certificate from their trade organisation. As a result of this decree, practically all the men joined a trade organisation, and, as every trade organisation is controlled by the Bolsheviks, the Bolsheviks in this way got more men under their power.

The "category" people can only go to municipal shops (as a matter of fact, all other shops are closed). The latest prices of goods in Petrograd were: bread 1 r. 50 c. a lb. at a municipal shop, but 20 roubles a lb. if bought outside (from Red Guards, sackmen, &c.); butter 75 roubles a lb. if bought outside—no fats of any description sold at municipal shops; sugar, which was only available about once a month, 1 r. 50 c. a lb. at municipal shops, and otherwise 80 roubles. Meat was sometimes obtainable at the market; as a matter of fact, it was supposed to be sold by card system, but it was generally sold in an underhand manner at the market. Beef 23 roubles a lb.; veal 26 roubles; pork 45 roubles. Meat was also obtainable from the sackmen. The Bolsheviks try to stop these sackmen, who go from house to house selling food.

The category people do not get their supplies regularly, or the full amount they are entitled to. The Supply Committee publishes in the paper from day to day what food is available, and what each category is allotted.

It is very difficult to draw any large amount of money out of a bank. The Bolsheviks allow 1,000 roubles a month to be taken out from an account, but even this has become more difficult lately, as they have just issued a decree that a man must get either his House Committee or some other

Bolshevik organisation to state that he is really in need of money. But by means of bribery, men draw out hundreds of thousands of roubles. All the banks have been nationalised, and now they are centralised. A decree was published a little while ago saying that, if a man had an account in three or four banks, he must choose one bank, and put all his money into that. If this decree was not obeyed, the Bolsheviks simply took all his money away. By this means the Bolsheviks can tell exactly how much money each man has.

If a new account was opened on the 1st January, 1918, the depositor was allowed, in principle, to draw out his money freely; but in practice this was not so. When the banks were nationalised new money could be taken out as desired (again only in principle). But when, about six weeks ago, the new decree about centralising all accounts was published, the position of affairs was altered. For example, if a man had 5,000 roubles in his new account, and 100,000 roubles in his old account, he could transfer his old account to his new account, so making 105,000 roubles in all. But, according to this decree, he was only allowed to draw to the amount of 5,000 roubles, as the old account was considered "barred." For transferring an account from one bank to another the commissars charged 25 per cent.

There are frequent strikes in factories, which often have to be put down by force. About six weeks ago there was a strike in the Putilof works. Trotski in a speech made a definite threat to use force if the men did not go back. As a result of this the strike was settled with only a few arrests taking place.

About two months ago there was an election for the Workmen's Committee in the Putilof Works, and this resulted in a majority for the Social Revolutionaries. The Bolsheviks would not consent to this, and there had to be another election. This shows that, in spite of the Workmen's Committees, the Bolsheviks are really in control. If the workmen get too independent, the Government simply closes the factory down; and if the Committee is troublesome the same thing happens, unless a new Committee is appointed. All members of the Committee have to be Communists, or in sympathy with the Communists. Often a factory has to close down for lack of fuel or certain machinery, but the men who are thus thrown out of work are given an unemployment allowance.

Mr. E— was a member of his House Committee in order to get put into the second category. The chief duties of the House Committee are to see that the different decrees of the Bolsheviks are carried out. If these are not carried out the Committee is held responsible, and is either fined or imprisoned. The Committee is forced to buy one newspaper a day in order to follow the decrees, as the Bolsheviks only publish their decrees in the newspaper. By this means practically everyone has to read the papers, and as only Bolshevik papers are allowed to be published their propaganda is seen by everyone.

All the streets are deserted, and there is no life at all. The Nevski is practically empty, and most of the shops are shut. But perfect order reigns in the streets; there is no looting or robbery.

There are hardly any executions now. This is due to the fact that the people's spirit has been broken, and that they now offer no opposition.

All restaurants are closed, with the exception of municipal restaurants and cafés. In an ordinary café a cup of tea, without milk or sugar, costs 1 rouble, and coffee, 3 r. 50 c.

Services still continue to be held in the churches, and on the whole they are well attended. The congregation is chiefly composed of women, but on the Russian New Year's Eve there were many men there. The priests, who used to be in the fourth category, are now in no category at all.

In Mr. E—'s opinion Allied intervention would be very welcome. He thinks 50,000 troops would be ample, and that the Bolsheviks would not be able to rouse any opposition against us. In fact, the Red Guard officers would be among the first to join our ranks. Everybody is hoping and praying that the Allies will intervene, and they would be welcomed with open arms everywhere.

Russians crossing the border from Russia into Finland are now, in the majority of cases, sent back to Russia again, unless they have some very strong influence in Finland itself.

Mr. F—, who has returned from Vladimir, states that he had his factory going right up to the day of his departure from — on the 6th February.

Before the revolution the output was:—
        1,100 poods (roughly 400 cwt.) yarn daily.
        800 pieces cloth.
The latest figures were for January 1919:—
        550 poods (roughly 200 cwt.) yarn daily.
        500 pieces cloth.

Out of 6,500 workmen there were not 200 convinced Bolsheviks. The majority were kept in order by pure terrorism, of which there were many examples within a radius of 40 versts of M——. When peasants refused to supply grain and cattle, and rose to protect their property, a Bolshevik force soon appeared in the neighbourhood, and if any resistance was offered, the whole village was wiped out. Usually, the peasants gave in at the first shot, a number of ringleaders would then be shot on the spot, and a number would be taken off to Moscow to prison.

Typhus is rapidly spreading in the country and the capitals. The average number of cases taken off trains arriving at the Kazan Station, Moscow, is twenty per train. At the Kursk Station in Moscow, typhus cases lie about the waiting halls. The hospitals are so full that patients are left in the corridor.

In places where people congregate, such as railway stations, market places, &c., the sanitary conditions are terrible. With the thawing of the snow the epidemic, which has reached enormous proportions during the winter frosts, will naturally increase in violence.

The Kazan railway runs one passenger train each

way to Kazan. This railway used to bring 40 per cent. of the food into Moscow. It now runs an average of three goods trains each way per day.

No one wants to join the Red Army now except the worst elements of the people. If a conscript deserts in the town where he joins, his parents or wife are treated with extreme brutality, sometimes being shot. But desertion often takes place while troops are going to the "front." Under these latter circumstances, the Bolsheviks are unable to trace their relations, so they are not touched.

Mr. F— considers one of the inducements to fight is that if the Red Army breaks through the enemy it usually finds large stores of food.

The progress of Bolshevism in Russia

Memorandum by Mr. B—.

THERE has now been time for considerable organisation of the Bolshevik Government. Russia has been
divided into four Federal Republics:—

    (1.) Commune of the North.

    (2.) Commune of the West.

    (3.) Central Commune.

    (4.) Commune of the Volga.

The first is composed of the Governments of
Petrograd, Archangel, Viatka, Vologda, part of the

Government of Pskov, Novgorod, Tcherepovetz and Olonetz.

The second comprises the Governments of Vitebsk, Smolensk and Pskov.

The third the Governments of Moscow, Orel, Koursk, Toula, Tver, Nijni-Novgorod, Voronege.

The fourth those of Kazan, Simbirsk, Saratov and Perm.

Each town is provided with its Council of Deputies and its Commission for fighting counter-revolution, sabotage and speculation. Each district besides has its Council of Deputies (Sovdep) and its Extraordinary Commission. These institutions direct all local affairs, but they are all subject to the authority of the Central Executive Committee, which sits at Moscow. The pan-Russian Extraordinary Commission against counter-revolution, &c., also sits at Moscow. The members of these bodies are supposed to be elected by the pan-Russian Congress of Workmen, Peasants, Red Guards, Sailors and Cossack Deputies; foreign affairs are under the exclusive management of George Tchitcherine. The Central Committee is composed as follows:—

Lenin	President.
Trotsky	Military and Naval Commissary.
Tchitcherine	Foreign Affairs.
Spiez	Commissary of Labour.
Podrovski	Interior (ex-Professor of History at Moscow).
Lounatcharski	Education.

Nevski	Commissary of Roads and Communications. A former engineer at the Ministry.
Oulianova	Lenin's wife, social assistant.
Stoutchka	Justice. Formerly a Deputy of the Petrograd Tribunal.
Tziouroupa	Minister of Food.
Bontch-Brouevitch	Business Manager.

On the 25th October, 1918, the Bolshevik troops of Petrograd and the neighbourhood numbered hardly more than two divisions. Regimental committees have been abolished throughout the Army, and the power was transferred to military commissaries, who were charged with attending to the political *moral*. The Bolsheviks have neglected no means for increasing the number of their troops. Disabled soldiers of the old Army released from Germany are concentrated on their arrival either at Petrograd or Moscow and quartered with soldiers of the Red Guard. They are left without clothing, with insufficient rations, and without medical attendance, while the Red Guard, with whom they are mingled, is well fed, clothed, and amply supplied with money. When they complain, the answer is: "Enrol in the Red Guard." Refractory cases are cruelly treated. At the head of the Red Guard is a former colonel of the staff, a Lett named Vatatis. Each soldier receives 300 to 500 roubles a month, equipment, food on a higher scale than all the other categories, and a promise to support his family in the event of death; but, in spite of their privileged situation, the Red Guard have not the confidence of the Government, and, as intercepted letters show, many of them are disaffected. The real reliance of the Government is placed in the "International Battalions of the Army," which are formed of Letts and Chinese, who are used as punitive companies both in the Army and in the interior. Theoretically, the International Battalions are on an equality with the Red Guard, but actually they are far better paid, and they can count on absolute immunity for the excesses they commit against the wretched civil population which is left at their mercy. There is compulsory military instruction in the towns for all men between 17 and 40, in the form of drills twice a week. While its cohesion lasts, the Bolshevik Army is an incontestable force.

All assemblies except those organised by the Bolsheviks are forbidden in the towns. Anti-Bolshevik meetings are dispersed by armed force and their organisers shot. No Press exists except the Bolshevik Press. The Bolsheviks organise Sunday reunions, in which such subjects as, "Should one enrol in the Red Guards?"; "Who will give us our daily bread?"; "The world revolution," &c., are debated.

So effective is the Terror that no one dares to engage in anti-Bolshevik propaganda. People have been arrested for a simple telephonic conversation, in which the terms seemed ambiguous or could be interpreted as adverse to the Bolsheviks. An arrest is the prelude to every kind of corruption; the rich have to pay huge exactions to intermediaries, who are usually Jews, before they can obtain their release.

Latterly "mass arrests" have come into fashion. It was thought at first that these were ordered by the Extraordinary Commission against counter-revolution, but it is now known that they are ordered by a special Revolutionary Committee called for short "the Three," because it consists of three members. This committee is independent of the Extraordinary Commission and is controlled only by the Commissary of War. Persons arrested by its orders have never been seen again.

The proceedings of this committee are kept secret; its very composition is unknown to the public.

It has already been mentioned that the Red Guard is disaffected. A letter from a sailor named Borzof, written on the eve of going to the front, says, "The authorities seem to think that we are going to support the interests of the Soviets, but they are greatly mistaken. All the sailors are otherwise inclined ... many of them go simply to avoid hunger ... I think there will be an end to all this very soon; the Allies will overpower us." Another letter from Petrograd says, "We hear that Petrograd, before any other Russian town, will be in touch with Europe, but in the meantime half the inhabitants there are dying from hunger and typhoid fever." These letters and others were sent by the Russian Censor to the Extraordinary Commission for fighting the counter-revolution, and no doubt the writers have already been dealt with in the usual way.

There is, of course, in Russia a public opinion quite outside the Bolsheviks—an opinion which

longs ardently for any kind of intervention—Allied or
German—which which will put an end to the
present state of anarchy. So far it has expressed itself
only in half-hearted insurrections, as for example that
of Yaroslav and the assassination of Mirbach, &c.
Nevertheless, in spite of the apparent stability of the
Bolshevik Government, in spite of the ineptitude of
its opponents, there are signs that the Terrorist
Oligarchy is tottering. It is indeed impossible to
believe that a Government, financially bankrupt and
unable to feed its population, can survive for very
long, however drastically it attempts to govern by terror. A neutral in Petrograd said recently that hatred
towards the Government and everybody connected
with it is spreading among all classes of the population, including peasants and the working men. The
end will probably come quite suddenly, as it did in
the French Terror.

The anti-Bolshevik parties are considering all
sorts of devices for discrediting the Bolsheviks. One is
to flood the country with false currency, in order to
throw discredit on the Soviets; another, to seize the
printing office, where bank notes are produced, at
Petrograd; another, to obtain employment in
Government offices for the purpose of furnishing
information to their Party, which is being conducted
by Boris Asvinkof. Even the working class of the two
capitals is divided and there is a considerable anti-
Bolshevik party. The general opinion of the educated
classes is that a force of half a million would suffice to
overthrow the Bolsheviks with very few losses.

One is startled from time to time by hearing that some well-known man of education has joined the Bolsheviks, such for instance as Maxim Gorki and the famous singer Chaliapin. The fact is that there are many specious things in the Bolshevik creed designed to capture persons of all shades of opinion. It is not usually with the principles of a system of Government that fault can be found, but in the application of the principles, and when these are applied by ruffians, such as the Terrorists of the French and the Russian Revolutions, the principles fall into ruin. Rose-coloured accounts of the Bolshevik régime are written by persons who have only the principles to go by. Take, for example, the housing question. Some families have more rooms than they can live in, others have to live in one room, others again have no room at all. The Bolshevik Government commandeers a large house and lets it to indigent persons, so that all have equal housing accommodation. The house is managed by a committee and the only person who dislikes the arrangement is the owner of the house.

Much is made among the Bolshevik sympathisers in England of the Bolshevik system of public education, but it is easy to acquire merit for any educational system in a country where there was practically no elementary education before the revolution. It is also true that the opera and the theatres are kept running, but I am assured that the opera performed to an empty house until the Government gave orders that it was to be filled. Such methods of window dressing are not unknown in other countries.

Other reports show that Bolshevism is still a potent force in Siberia and that Bolsheviks are in close touch with those in European Russia.

In destroying the fabric of society the Bolsheviks appear to be adopting the methods of "skyscrapers" in New York, which is to dig out everything to a depth of 300 ft. in order to erect a new and stable edifice. They have said more than once that unless they can by propaganda induce a sympathetic revolution in other countries their fate must be sealed; and the fever of propaganda which now possesses them is really a measure of self-preservation.

It is now reported that they are abandoning propaganda by leaflets in favour of personal and secret propaganda.

The progress of Bolshevism abroad
Memorandum by Mr. B——.

FROM a report recently received from a former Russian statesman, it certainly appears that Bolshevism is dying at its roots. He says that the split between the Lenin and Trotsky group has become menacing. The few idealists that still remain among the Bolsheviks are seeing their ideas falling to pieces one after another, while a world revolution is still hanging fire. The leaders, who have full details of the position of Bolshevism both in Russia and abroad, clearly foresee their downfall, and admit their discouragement in private conversation with their friends. The "middle" Bolsheviks, *i.e.*, the Commissars, Soviet staff, and officers of the Red

Army, knowing nothing of the progress of events except what they read in the Bolshevik press, are less dismayed. They still believe in the eventual victory of Bolshevism in Germany, and are looking forward to disturbances in England, but many of them are already looking out for hiding places, and it is believed that they will desert the Bolsheviks as soon as there is another revolution.

The minor Bolsheviks, Communist workmen, &c., are not concerned with politics at all. Their sole preoccupation is the question of food. Those who are living at the Smolny seem to be convinced of the early downfall of the Soviet Government, owing to disorganisation in the Red Army, revolts in the villages, and famine. Many of them are returning to their homes and throwing off the mask of Bolshevism. The mass of the townspeople are terrorised and incapable of any independent action.

Under-feeding is having its effect, and the epidemics of typhus, small-pox, and influenza are spreading rapidly. In the Obuchof hospital, during December, the mortality amounted to 14,000. During that month the population of Petrograd fell by 105,000. Next to disease and famine, the absence of fuel is the worst scourge. All this presses terribly upon the prisoners, who are now thrust eight into a cell intended for one person, and fed upon putrid herrings and soup made from potato peel. Typhoid, small-pox, and influenza cases are left in the same cell with un-infected persons, and in the quarantine cells eight to ten patients lie together.

There is complete disorganisation of transport. The Bolsheviks are doing all they can to postpone the day of complete breakdown by giving superior diet to the railway workers, who are very discontented.

The Red Army continues to hold together, but its *moral* is said to have declined. The *moral* of the fleet is in a dangerous state. Many of the sailors have amassed a fortune during the past year, and they believe that they can only retain it by bringing in a bourgeois Government. They are now not only discontented, but anti-Bolshevik. In the beginning of January they demanded the removal of commissars from the ships, which was done. An attempt made by the Government to send the sailors to the front was disastrous. They refused to go, and refused to be disarmed. The relations between the sailors and officers have lately improved, and the Bolshevik leaders are aware of the danger of having in the very centre of Petrograd a compact armed force hostile to them. All that the sailors need for taking action is a leader.

There is no Labour question in Petrograd because there are no capitalists, no trade, and no industry. The workmen, who used to number hundreds of thousands, may now be counted in thousands. Many of them have taken service under the Bolsheviks, and are employed in various commissariats and committees. Large numbers have drifted away into the country. On the whole, those who remain are against the Bolsheviks. They control the water supply, the electric, fire stations, the tramways, and arsenal. They appear to entertain no ill-feeling towards the *bourgeoisie*, but, on the other hand, they are quite inarticulate as to the form of Government they would prefer.

At the Putilof works anti-Semitism is growing, probably because the food supply committees are entirely in the hands of Jews—and voices can be heard sometimes calling for a "pogrom."

In the railway workshops the men are split into two parties—Bolshevik and anti-Bolshevik. The Government is carrying on a feverish propaganda among them, but without much effect. The women-folk are specially counter-revolutionary, probably because they feel the want of food more severely. The workmen are generally opposed to the Red Army and against war of any kind.

The food supply, in which there was a temporary improvement during January, has again become hopeless. In Petrograd there is no reserve of food.

The peasants in the Northern governments are generally anti-Bolshevik, but the feeling varies in the different governments, and is most hostile where requisitions have been made. The "Committees of the Poor" are avoided by respectable peasants. Members of those committees—numbering sometimes 20 per cent. of the population—do no work and live at the expense of the local peasants by requisition. This led to revolts in January in several districts. Nearly all the peasants are armed, some even having machine guns and a supply of cartridges. They have ceased to take the slightest interest in politics. What they need is cloth and iron, as well as food.

The most interesting feature in the report is the statement that, both in the towns and villages, there is a reawakening of religion. At Kolpin the churches are overcrowded; the propaganda of Ivan Tchirikof is meeting with success; Pashkovtsef's sect is growing, and new sects are appearing. In the villages also the priests are no longer molested and are beginning to reopen the churches.

At the International Communist Conference at Moscow, according to the Russian wireless, Kamenef declared for the doctrines of Karl Marx and a proletarian dictatorship. Lenin spoke hopefully of the victory of the Social Revolution being secured. "In spite," he said, "of all the obstacles and the number of victims who may suffer in the progress of the cause, we may live to see a universal Republic of Soviets." There was to be a review of the Red Army for the edification of the foreign delegates.

The Red Army is flooded with propaganda literature, and Trotsky is conducting a series of mass meetings. The propaganda trains are decorated fantastically in order to make an impression on the soldiers. Trotsky's present theme is the coming of the Socialistic State. Stoppage of work in factories is almost universal, not only from the lack of fuel, but from strikes.

The Russian wireless has issued a statement that the Government, although not recognising the Berne Conference as representative of the working classes, will allow the Commission to travel through Russia, just as they would allow any bourgeois Commission to do the same, but they enquire whether the Governments of the various countries' representatives will allow a Bolshevik Commission to inspect their countries.

A man named J——, who has arrived in Norway from Russia, states that he was employed as engineer at a printing works. In the spring of 1918 the press was taken over by the Soviet Government, and was employed in printing propaganda in many languages —"Every language," he says, "except Russian." Most of the matter printed was in German, but there was a good deal of English too, as well as leaflets in Asiatic languages, for which purpose type was purchased in India. He specially remembered Sanscrit and Hindustani.

The efforts of the Bolsheviks to corrupt the Allied soldiers at Archangel are reported to be futile. Specimens of the literature dropped by Bolshevik aeroplanes comprised English translations of mani-festoes by Lenin and Petrof, a man who was charged in connection with the Houndsditch murders.

There are many reports about the printing of forged notes for the various Allied countries, and the £1 note is reported to be forged in enormous quan-tities. The only forged notes now being circulated in this country are very crude, and are quite unworthy of the style of note printing for which the Russians used to be famous. Most of the forgery has been badly executed by hand on inferior paper.

EXTRACTS FROM THE RUSSIAN PRESS

Extract from the "Krasnaya Gazeta" (Organ of Red Army), September 1, 1918.
ARTICLE, entitled "Blood for Blood," begins in the following way:—

"We will turn our hearts into steel, which we will temper in the fire of suffering and the blood of fighters for freedom. We will make our hearts cruel, hard, and immovable, so that no mercy will enter them, and so that they will not quiver at the sight of a sea of enemy blood. We will let loose the floodgates of that sea. Without mercy, without sparing, we will kill our enemies in scores of hundreds. Let them be thousands; let them drown themselves in their own blood. For the blood of Lenin and Uritski, Zinovief, and Volodarski, let there be floods of the blood of the bourgeois—more blood, as much as possible."

Extracts from Official Journal ("Izvestiya"), September 1918.

THERE are only two possibilities—the dictatorship of the bourgeoisie or the dictatorship of the proletariat ... The proletariat will reply to the attempt on Lenin in a manner that will make the whole bourgeoisie shudder with horror.

Assassination at Petrograd of Kommissar Uritsky by Kannegisser Jew Dvoryanin, twenty-two years of age, student, formerly Junker of Artillery School.

"Krasnaya Gazeta" writes: "Whole bourgeoisie must answer for this act of terror ... Thousands of our enemies must pay for Uritsky's death ... We must teach bourgeoisie a bloody lesson ... Death to the bourgeoisie."

ATTEMPT ON LENIN.
Proclamation Issued by the Extraordinary Commission and signed "Peters"

PROCLAMATION states that "the criminal hand of a member of the Social-Revolutionary Party, directed by the Anglo-French, has dared to fire at the leader of the working class." This crime will be answered by a "massive terror." Woe to those who stand in the path of the working class. All representatives of capital will be sent to forced labour, and their property confiscated. Counter-revolutionaries will be exterminated and crushed beneath the heavy hammer of the revolutionary proletariat.

Petrovsky, Kommissar for Interior, issues circular telegraphic order reproving local Soviets for their "extraordinarily insignificant number of serious repressions and mass shootings of White Guards and bourgeoisie." An immediate end must be put to these grandmotherly methods. All Right Social-Revolutionaries must be immediately arrested. Considerable numbers of hostages must be taken from bourgeoisie and former officers. At the slightest attempt at resistance, or the slightest movement in White Guard circles, mass shootings of hostages must be immediately employed. Indecisive and irresolute action in this matter on the part of local Soviets will be severely dealt with.

TERRORISM.

THE Council of the People's Commissaries, having considered the report of the chairman of the Extraordinary Commission, found that under the existing conditions it was most necessary to secure the safety of the rear by means of terror. To strengthen the activity of the Extraordinary Commission, and render it more systematic, as many responsible party comrades as possible are to be sent to work on the Commission. The Soviet Republic must be made secure against its class enemies by sending them to concentration camps.

All persons belonging to White Guard organisations or involved in conspiracies and rebellions are to be shot. Their names and the particulars of their cases are to be published.

("Northern Commune," September 9, 1918.)

Tver, 9th September.—The Extraordinary Commission has arrested and sent to concentration camps over 130 hostages from among the bourgeoisie. The prisoners include members of the Cadet party, Socialist-Revolutionaries of the Right, former officers, well-known members of the propertied classes and policemen.

("Northern Commune," September 10, 1918.)

Jaroslav, 9th September.—In the whole of the Jaroslav Government a strict registration of the bourgeoisie and its partisans has been organised. Manifestly anti-Soviet elements are being shot; suspected persons are interned in concentration camps; non-working sections of the population are subjected to compulsory labour.

("Northern Commune," September 10, 1918.)

Atkarsk, 11th September.—Yesterday martial law was proclaimed in the town. Eight counter-revolutionaries were shot.

("Northern Commune," September 12, 1918.)

Borisoglebsk, 16th September.—For an attempt to organise a movement in opposition to the Soviet power, nine local counter-revolutionaries were shot, namely—two rich land-owners, six merchants and the local "Corn King" Vasiliev.

("Northern Commune," September 16, 1918.)

Resolution passed by the Soviet of the First Urban District of Petrograd:—

" ... The meeting welcomes the fact that mass terror is being used against the White Guards and higher bourgeois classes, and declares that every attempt on the life of any of our leaders will be answered by the proletariat by shooting down not only of hundreds, as is the case now, but of thousands of White Guards, bankers, manufacturers, Cadets (constitutional democrats) and Socialist-Revolutionaries of the Right."

("Northern Commune," September 18, 1918.)

In Astrakhan the Extraordinary Commission has shot ten Socialist-Revolutionaries of the Right involved in a plot against the Soviet power. In Karamyshef a priest named Lubimof and a deacon named Kvintil have been shot for revolutionary agitation against the decree separating the Church from the State, and for an appeal to overthrow the Soviet Government. In Perm, in retaliation for the assassination of Uritzky and for the attempt on Lenin, fifty hostages from among the bourgeois classes and the White Guards were shot (a few names are given). In Sebesh a priest named Kirkevich was shot for counter-revolutionary propaganda, and for having said masses for the late Nicholas Romanov.

("Northern Commune," September 18, 1918.)

The following telegram has been received from the Cavalry Corps Staff:—

"Additional arrests have been made in connection with the affair of former officers and Civil Service officials involved in preparing a rising in Vologda. When the plot was discovered they fled to Archangel and to Murmansk. The prisoners were caught disguised as peasants; all had forged papers on them. The political department of the Corps has in its possession receipts for sums of money received by the arrested persons from the British through Colonel Kurtenkof. In connection with this affair fifteen have been shot, mostly military men. Among them were General Astashof, Military Engineer Bodrovolsky, Captain Nikitin and two Socialist-Revolutionaries of the Left—Sudotin and Tourba. Apart from these, the Commander of the Expeditionary Detachment, the sailor Shimansky, who was not equal to the situation, was also shot.

("Northern Commune," September 19, 1918.)

"To overcome our enemies we must have our own Socialist Militarism. We must win over to our side 90 millions out of the 100 millions of population of Russia under the Soviets. As for the rest, we have nothing to say to them; they must be annihilated."

(Speech by Zinoviev; reported in the "Northern Commune," September 19, 1918.)

The work of the Extraordinary Commission is most responsible and calls for the greatest restraint of their members. Do they possess this restraint? Unfortunately, I cannot discuss here whether and how far all the arrests and executions carried out in various places by the Extraordinary Commissions were really necessary. On this point there are differences of opinion in the party ... The absence of the necessary restraint makes one feel appalled at the "instruction" issued by the All-Russian Extraordinary Commission to "All Provincial Extraordinary Commissions," which says:— "The All-Russian Extraordinary Commission is perfectly independent in its work, carrying out house searches, arrests, executions, of which it afterwards reports to the Council of the People's Commissaries and to the Central Executive Council." Further, the Provincial and District Extraordinary Commissions "are independent in their activities, and when called upon by the local Executive Council present a report of their work." In so far as house searches and arrests are concerned, a report made afterwards may result in putting right irregularities committed owing to lack of restraint. The same cannot be said of executions ... It can also be seen from the "instruction" that personal safety is to a certain extent guaranteed only to members of the Government, of the Central Executive Council and of the local Executive Committees. With the exception of these few persons all members of the local committees of the (Bolshevik) party, of the Control Committees and of the Executive Committee of the party may be shot at any time by the decision of any Extraordinary Commission of a small district town if they happen to be on its territory, and a report of that made afterwards.

(From an article by M. Alminsky, "Pravda," October 8, 1918.)

Comrade Bokif gave details of the work of the Petrograd District Commission since the evacuation of the All-Russian Extraordinary Commission to Moscow. The total number of arrested persons was 6,220. 800 were shot.

(From a report of a meeting of the Conference of the Extraordinary Commission, "Izvestiya," October 19, 1918, No. 228.)

A riot occurred in the Kirsanof district. The rioters shouted, "Down with the Soviets." They dissolved the Soviet and the Committee of the Village Poor. The riot was suppressed by a detachment of the Soviet troops. Six ringleaders were shot. The case is under examination.

("Izvestiya," November 5, 1918.)

By order of the Military Revolutionary Committee of Petrograd several officers were shot for spreading untrue rumours that the Soviet authority had lost the confidence of the people.

All relatives of the officers of the 86th Infantry Regiment (which deserted to the Whites) were shot.

("Northern Commune" (quoted from "Russian Life" (Helsingfors)), March 11, 1919.)

TREATMENT OF THE BOURGEOISIE.

Orel.—To-day the Orel bourgeoisie commenced compulsory work to which it was made liable. Parties of the bourgeoisie, thus made to work, are cleaning the streets and squares from rubbish and dirt.

("Izvestiya," October 19, 1918, No. 288.)

Chembar.—The bourgeoisie put to compulsory work is repairing the pavements and the roads.

("Pravda," October 6, 1918, No. 205.)

If you come to Petrograd you will see scores of bourgeoisie laying the pavement in the courtyard of the Smolny ... I wish you could see how well they unload coal on the Neva and clean the barracks.

(From a speech by Zinoviev, "Pravda," October 11, 1918, No. 219.)

Large forces of mobilised bourgeoisie have been sent to the front to do trench work.

("Krasnaya Gazeta," October 16, 1918.)

A Camp for the Bourgeoisie.

THE District Extraordinary Commission (Saransk) has organised a camp of concentration for the local bourgeoisie and kulaki (the close-fisted).

The duties of the confined shall consist in keeping clean the town of Saransk.

The existence of the camp will be maintained at the expense of the same bourgeoisie.

("Krasnaya Gazeta" (The Red Gazette),
Petrograd, November 6, 1918, No. 237.)

DESERTIONS FROM THE RED ARMY.

The Fight against Desertion.

THE "Goios Krasnoarmeytza" (Voice of the Red Armyman), of the 2nd February, issued at Yamburg by the Sixth Light Infantry Division, contains the following announcement:—

"In view of the mass desertions of Red Army men and the necessity of putting a stop to those citizens agitating among them against Soviet authority, and spreading among them false rumours, causing panic among the army and in the rear, and also concealing deserters, persons who are in reality agents of Anglo-French capital, such persons are subject to arrest and to delivery to trial by the Military Revolutionary Tribunal as enemies of the workers' and peasants' government.

"All town, district, and village Soviets of the frontal zone of the Yamburg district and of the neighbouring districts are instructed by the military Soviet of the division and by the Yamburg district Executive Committee to bring to the immediate notice of the Military Revolutionary Tribunal all cases of wandering Red Army men, to detain all persons spreading false rumours, to arrest private persons as well as Red Army men detected in selling or buying military arms and munitions, and to place on all roads barrier-guards and patrols for the apprehension of deserters.

"The Military Revolutionary Tribunal brings to the notice of Red Army men that the time for words and exhortation has passed, and that the time has come demanding the conscious performance of the tasks of the Soviet Republic.

"The concealment and the misplaced solicitude of workmen and peasants in relation to deserters are abetting the licentiousness and idleness in the ranks of the Red Army.

"A deserter needs neither bread nor a refuge, but a bullet.

"Bread and a refuge are due only to the proletariat Red Army.

"(The Military Revolutionary Tribunal at the Front.)"

BOLSHEVISM AND SOCIAL DEMOCRACY.
Arrest of the Labour Conference.
AN open letter of the delegates, kept in the Moscow Taganka Prison, to all citizens:—

"We, members of the Labour Conference, representing independent working-class organisations of various towns of Russia (Petrograd, Moscow, Tula, Sormova, Kolomna, Kulebaki, Tver, Nijni-Novgorod, Vologda, Bezshiza, Orel, Votkinski Zavod), arrested at our second meeting, on the 23rd July, in the

'Co-operation Hall,' feel it our public duty to protest before all citizens of Russia, against the false and calumnious reports published by the Bolshevik Government press on the 27th and 28th July. The Bolshevik Government takes advantage of the fact that it has muzzled the whole independent press and that we, members of the Labour Conference, are locked up in prison, under incredible conditions.

"Our Conference was not 'a secret counter-revolutionary plot organised by well-to-do people and intellectuals,' &c., but a public conference of delegates of working-class organisations, which was beforehand known to and discussed by the whole press, including that of the Bolsheviks.

"The delegates were sent to the Conference not by 'Menshevik or Socialist-Revolutionaries' groups' as falsely stated in the 'Izvestiya,' which desires to deceive workmen who have not yet deserted the Government, but by assemblies of delegates from works and factories who have tens of thousands of electors behind them. The adopted general basis of representation was one delegate for 5,000 workmen. The 'Izvestiya' goes so far as to state shamelessly that the delegates Polikarpof and Pushkin, sent by the Tula workmen, were elected by 60 or 160 men, whereas they were sent by the Tula assembly, which consisted of delegates elected by the majority of Tula workmen. At places where independent workmen's organisations could not yet be set up, delegates to the Conference were sent by individual big factories.

"Having calumniously described the delegates as

impostors who represent nobody, the 'Izvestiya'—
with the insolence characteristic of the organs of the
Tsarist régime—did not stop at giving false information about things found on the arrested delegates in
order to cast a shadow on their characters. Thus, it is
reported that Comrade Berg was found to be in possession of 6,000 roubles. As a matter of fact, he had
only 590 roubles. Comrade Leikin is stated to have
had 160 roubles, and he had in fact 1 rouble 65
kopecks. The 'Izvestiya' further states that on Leikin
the following things were found: a ring, diamonds,
and a gold watch, whereas all his 'jewellery' consisted
of an ordinary gun-metal watch, which it did not
occur even to the prison warders to take away.

"The Bolshevik Government has to resort to stu-
pid, shameless lies to justify the preposterous arrests of
the workmen's delegates who dared to show some
independent organising initiative.

"The conference of workmen's delegates was
convened to make arrangements for the convocation
of an All-Russian Labour Congress, and had held two
meetings. The agenda of the Conference included the
following items:— Measures against the disintegra-
tion of the working-class movement; what can be
done to effect a concentration of its forces and its
proper organisation; arrangements for the All-Russian
Labour Conference. But the Communist
Government, just as its Tsarist predecessors, do not
tolerate any symptoms of an independent working-
class movement, because it is this movement which
constitutes a menace to their power. In this

movement they see a reflection of the food crisis, and, incapable of solving the State problems which they have before them, they resort to repressive measures directed against the leaders of the working-class movement. Workmen's organisations are subjected to unheard-of repressions.

"Long live the working-class organisations!

"Long live their independence, their revolutionary and organising initiative!

"('Signed')—A.N. Smirnof, workman of the Cartridge Factory, delegate from Petrograd; N. N. Gliebof, workman of Poutilof Works; J. S. Leikin, delegate of the Assembly of Delegates of the Nijni and Vladimir districts. Workmen: D.V. Zakharof, secretary of a trade union; D. I. Zakharof, Sormovo; V. I. Matveef, Sormovo; A. A.Vezkalm, carpenter, member of the Executive Committee of the Lettish Social Democratic Party; I. G.Volkof, turner, member of the Executive Committee of the Petrograd Union of Metal Workers; A. A. Chinenkof, Nijni; S. P. Polikarpof, Tula; N. K. Borisenko, Petrograd Tube Works; V. G. Chirkin, turner, member of the All-Russian Council of Trade Unions; Berg, Electrical Works; D. Smirnof, Arsenal, Petrograd; Victor Alter, delegate of the Executive Committee of the 'Bund' (Jewish Socialist Party); Pushkin, workman of the Tula Small Arms Factory, &c."

> ("Workers' International" (organ of the
> Petrograd Committee of the Russian
> Social-Democratic Labour Party),
> August 7, 1918.)

The imaginary dictatorship of the proletariat has definitely turned into the dictatorship of the Bolshevik party, which attracted all sorts of adventurers and suspicious characters and is supported only by the naked force of hired bayonets. Their sham socialism resulted in the complete destruction of Russian industry, in the country's enslavement to foreign capital, in the destruction of all class organisations of the proletariat, in the suppression of all democratic liberty and of all organs of democratic State life, thus preparing the ground for a bourgeois counter-revolution of the worst and most brutal kind.

The Bolsheviks are unable to solve the food problem, and their attempt to bribe the proletariat by organising expeditions into the villages in order to seize supplies of bread drives the peasantry into the arms of the counter-revolution and threatens to rouse its hatred towards the town in general, and the proletariat in particular, for a long time to come ...

In continuing the struggle against the Bolshevik tyranny which dishonours the Russian revolution, social democracy pursues the following aims: (1) To make it impossible for the working class to have to shed its blood for the sake of maintaining the sham dictatorship of the toiling masses or of the sham socialistic order, both of which are bound to perish and are meanwhile killing the soul and body of the proletariat; (2) To organise the working-class into a force which, in union with other democratic forces of the country, will be able to throw off the yoke of the Bolshevik régime, to defend the democratic conquests of the revolution and to oppose any reactionary force which would attempt to hang a millstone around the neck of the Russian democracy ...

Forty delegates elected by workmen of various towns, to a conference, for the purpose of making arrangements for the convocation of a Labour Congress, have been arrested and committed for trial by the Supreme Revolutionary Tribunal, created to pass death sentences without the ordinary guarantees of a fair trial. They are falsely and calumniously accused of organising a counter-revolutionary plot. Among the arrested are the most prominent workers of the Social Democratic Labour movement, as, for instance, Abramovitch, member of the Central Executive Committees of the Russian Social Democratic Labour Party and of the "Bund," who is personally well-known to many foreign comrades; Alter, member of the Executive Committee of the "Bund"; Smirnof, member of last year's Soviet Delegation to the Western Countries; Vezkaln, member of the Executive Committee of the Lettish Social Democratic Party; Volkof, chairman of the Petrograd Union of Workmen's Co-operative Societies; Zakharof, secretary of the Petrograd Union of Workmen of Chemical Factories; and other prominent workers of the trade union and co-operative movement.

We demand immediate intervention of all Socialist parties to avert the shameful and criminal proceeding.

(Protest of the Social Democratic Labour Party and of the Jewish Socialist Party sent to the Executive Committees of all Socialist Parties of Europe and America, August, 1918.)

The Extraordinary Commission of the Union of Northern Communes at a meeting of October 22nd, considered the legal cases connected with the sailors' mutiny of October 14th. It was found on examination that the movement was organised by the Petrograd Committee of the Socialist Revolutionaries of the Left, the resolution passed by the sailors of the 2nd Baltic Squadron having been framed with the assistance of members of the above Committee, approved of by the Conference of the party, which sent its greetings to the sailors. Apart from this, the resolution was printed on a cyclostyle in the premises of the above Committee, which delegated their party agitators to the sailors' meeting. At the head of the organisation were thirteen persons. Two escaped. All the others were sentenced by the Extraordinary Commission to be shot.

("Izvestiya," October 31, 1918.)

By the decision of the Extraordinary Commission the Socialist-Revolutionary, Firsof, has been shot. Firsof was executed for writing and distributing leaflets in which the Socialist-Revolutionaries invited workmen to give allegiance to the Archangel Government.

("Northern Commune," September 18, 1918.)

The Extraordinary Commission of the Province has arrested the leading members of the local organisation of Left and Right Social Revolutionaries for the spreading of proclamations. In connection with the discovery of the plot, some Left Social Revolutionaries have been arrested in Moscow. An agitation has been conducted in the Red Army for the overthrow of Soviet authority. Proclamations were distributed calling for a struggle against Soviet authority, for the immediate organisation of committees and for the encouragement, through chosen commanders, of a campaign of terror against Trotsky and other prominent leaders of the Communist party. The agitation and the proclamations were without success. The responsible worker of the Kaluga Provisions Commissariat, the Left Social Revolutionary, Prigalin, was arrested. A rough draft of a proclamation, in the name of the party, calling for the overthrow of the Bolsheviks and the establishment of a coalition without the Bolsheviks, was found on him.

(Russian Wireless, February 22, 1919.)

The Tribunal dealing with Mme. Spiridonova (the leader of the Social Revolutionary party, who was recently arrested on a charge of conspiracy against the Soviet authority) has decided, in view of the abnormal state of mind of the accused, to isolate her from all political and social activity for the duration of a year.

Mme. Spiridonova is to be detained in a sanatorium, where she will be allowed facilities for recreation and intellectual work.

(Russian Wireless, February 26, 1919.)

Don't be like the "Old Masters."
In one of the Sunday numbers of the "Krasnaya Gazeta" there was an article by comrade Kuznetzof under the title "The Eleventh." In this article he recalled how arrogantly, how appallingly, the old masters conducted themselves toward working-men.

Yes, comrade Kuznetzof, it is unpleasant and humiliating to recall this gentry, but it is even more unpleasant and humiliating to meet the same kind of "old masters" at the present time. I know very many comrades who occupy various responsible posts in unions and committees, and when you happen to turn to them with some enquiry or request for co-operation, they are no better than the masters of the old régime: they answer either rudely and arrogantly, or they do not answer at all.

It is humiliating to see this at the present time. And I say to such comrades: "Don't be, if I may so express myself, like the 'old masters.' Go to meet the oppressed and the poor. Train yourselves in this spirit, and only then call yourselves Communists and protectors of the working man. Hands off, all those who do not act as they speak!"

([Letter from a Working Man.] "Krasnaya Gazeta" (The Red Gazette), Petrograd, October 29, 1918, No. 230.)

THE BOLSHEVIKS AND THE PRESS.

The Suppression of the Paper "Mir" (Peace).—In accordance with the decision published in the "Izvestiya" on the 27th July, No. 159, the Press Department granted permits to issue periodical publications which accepted the Soviet platform. When granting permissions, the Press Department took into consideration the available supplies of paper, whether the population was in need of the proposed periodical publication, and also the necessity of providing employment for printers and pressmen. Thus, permission was granted to issue the paper "Mir," especially in view of the publisher's declaration that the paper was intended to propagate pacifist ideas. At the present moment the requirements of the population of the Federal Socialist Republic for means of daily information are adequately met by the Soviet publications; employment for those engaged in journalistic work is secured in the Soviet papers; a paper crisis is approaching. The Press Department, therefore, considers it impossible to permit the further publication of the "Mir," ... and has decided to suppress this paper for ever.

("Izvestiya," October 17, 1918, No. 226.)

The Central Executive Committee has confirmed the decision to close the newspaper, "Vsegda Vperiod," as its appeals for the cessation of civil war appear to be a betrayal of the working-class.

(Russian Wireless, February 26, 1919.)

Compulsory Purchase of Newspapers.

To the Notice of the House Committees of Poverty.

ON 20th July of the present year there was published obligatory regulation No. 27, to the following effect:—

"Every house committee in the city of Petrograd and other towns, included in the Union of Communes of the Northern Region, is under obligation to subscribe, paying for same, to one copy of the newspaper, the "Northern Commune" (the official organ of the Soviets of the Northern Region).

"The newspaper should be given to every resident in the house on the first demand.

"Chairman of the Union of the Communes of the Northern region, Gr. Zinoviev.

"Commissary of printing, N. Kuzmin."

However, until now the majority of houses, inhabited pre-eminently by the bourgeoisie, do not fulfil the above-expressed obligatory regulation, and the working population of such houses is deprived of the possibility of receiving the "Northern Commune" in its house committees.

Therefore, the publishing office of the "Northern Commune" brings to the notice of all house committees that it has undertaken, through the medium of especial emissaries, the control of the fulfilment by house committees of the obligatory regulation No. 27, and all house committees which cannot show a receipt for a subscription to the newspaper, the "Northern Commune," will be immediately called to the most severe account for the breaking of the obligatory regulation.

Subscriptions will be received in the main office and branches of the "Northern Commune" daily, except Sundays and holidays, from 10 to 4.

> ("Severnaya Kommuna," Petrograd, November 10, 1918, No. 150.)

FREEDOM OF SPEECH.

AT the People's Court at Moscow was heard the case of Priest Filimonof, accused of circulating the book, "Who Governs Us."

In his book the author defamed the Soviet Government. The Court sentenced the reverend father ("batiushka") to ten years of public work.

> ("Krasnaya Gazeta" (The Red Gazette), Petrograd, October 10, 1918, No. 214.)

DECREE AS TO FREEDOM OF ASSOCIATION AND PUBLIC MEETINGS.

1. All societies, unions, and associations—political, economic, artistic, religious, &c.—formed on the territory of the Union of the Commune of the Northern Region must be registered at the corresponding Soviet or Committees of the village poor.

2. The constitution of the union or society, a list of founders and members of the committee, with names and addresses, and a list of all members, with their names and addresses, must be submitted at registration.

3. All books, minutes, &c., must always be kept at the disposal of representatives of the Soviet power for purposes of revision.

4. Three days' notice must be given to the Soviet, or to the Committee of the village poor, of all public and private meetings.

5. All meetings must be open to the representatives of the Soviet power, viz., the representatives of the Central and District Soviet, the Committee of the Poor, and the Kommandatur of the Revolutionary Secret Police Force (Okhrana).

6. Unions and societies which do not comply with those regulations will be regarded as counter-revolutionary organisations, and prosecuted.

("Northern Commune," September 13, 1918, No. 103.)

ECONOMIC CONDITIONS.

The Rise in Wages.

IN the last number of the "Narodnoye Khoziaystvo" (National Economy) are given the figures of the progress of wages in Russia during the decade of 1908–1918.

In general, wages have risen during the ten years from 1200 to 1300 per cent.

The highest rise has taken place in the textile industry, in which it has reached 1736 per cent. In the leather trade the wages have gone up in the same time 1501 per cent., in the colour printing industry 1440 per cent., in the writing paper industry 1434 per cent., in the metal and woodwork industries 1004 per cent., in the chemical industry 1069 per cent., and in the food products industry 1286 per cent.

It is necessary to remark that the greatest changes have occurred in those branches of industry which received smaller wages in previous years, as, for example, the textile industry. In this connection the wages of the women workers have risen relatively far in excess of those of the men workers. In the leather industry they have reached a 2500 per cent. increase, in the textile industry 2127 per cent.

("Pravda," Moscow, October 24, 1918, No. 230.)

The Commissariat of Food.

THE Food Commissariat of the Petrograd Workers' Commune informs the population that in February the adult population and children of all ages will be able to obtain on the presentation of their food cards (Coupon 14):—

      1st category.—1 lb. of sand sugar.

      2nd category.—$\frac{1}{2}$ lb. of sand sugar.

("Severnaya Kommuna," Petrograd, February 6, 1919.)

Ostashkof.

IN consequence of a complete absence of groats, white flour, and milk products, children suffer immensely. The mortality is great.

("Izvestiya," November 2, 1918, No. 240.)

Health.

IN the districts of the Viatka Government Spanish sickness is raging. There is no medical help, no drugs

are available. The population, frightend by the high
mortality, asks for help. There is an epidemic of grippe
in Sitnir Volost; 200 have died. Good agitators are
urgently required.

("Izvestiya," October 31, 1918.)

Disease: Eruptive typhus.
LAST week there were 967 registered cases of eruptive typhus in Petrograd, as against 820 registered
cases the previous week.

("Izvestiya," Moscow, February 7, 1919,
No. 28 (580).)

From an analysis of the "Krasnaya Gazeta" (The Red
Gazette), Petrograd, we get the following facts:—

In the issue of October 10, 1918, there are 39
advertisements. Of these, 23 deal with syphilis
treatment.

In the issue of October 11 there are 33 advertisements. Of these, 18 deal with syphilis treatment.

Of the 36 advertisements in the issue of October
16, 18 deal with syphilis.

Of the 42 advertisements in the issue of
November 6, 25 deal with syphilis and other venereal
diseases.

Requisitions.
AT a plenary sitting of the Soviet of Workers'
Deputies of the city region, in connection with
events in Germany, a resolution was passed in favour
of sending a greeting to the German proletariat, and

promise of being in readiness for sending assistance in the form of arms and food.

In connection with this, in view of the fact that this question is inevitably bound up with the security of our Red Army, the Soviet has decided to take the measure of requisitioning warm things belonging to the bourgeoisie for the Red Army.

("Krasnaya Gazeta" (The Red Gazette),
Petrograd, October 11, 1918, No. 215.)

The collection of warm things without the 1,000-rouble fine has been prolonged until October 20, inclusive.

("Krasnaya Gazeta" (The Red Gazette),
Petrograd, October 16, 1918, No. 219.)

Compulsory Labour for Hawkers, Cabmen, &c.
WITHIN a few days a registration will be made of all hawkers, cabmen, and unemployed of both sexes.

All these persons will be summoned to do urgent work caused by special conditions.

("Krasnaya Gazeta" (The Red Gazette),
Petrograd, November 2, 1918, No. 234.)

The Central Committee of the Revolutionary Communist Party informs all party organisations that all responsible workmen, Ukrainians, Letts, White Russians, and comrades of other nationalities, will be freed from their local labours, and sent to their own country only by permission of the Central

Committee. All secondary workmen will be freed by permission of the local organisations if their departure from their posts does not involve a breakdown of the local work.

(Russian Wireless, February 5, 1919.)

Other titles in the series

John Profumo and Christine Keeler, 1963

"The story must start with Stephen Ward, aged fifty. The son of a clergyman, by profession he was an osteopath … his skill was very considerable and he included among his patients many well-known people … Yet at the same time he was utterly immoral."

The Backdrop
The beginning of the '60s saw the publication of 'Lady Chatterley's Lover' and the dawn of sexual and social liberation as traditional morals began to be questioned and in some instances swept away.

The Book
In spite of the recent spate of political falls from grace, the Profumo Affair remains the biggest scandal ever to hit British politics. The Minister of War was found to be having an affair with a call girl who had associations with a Russian naval officer at the height of the Cold War. There are questions of cover-up, lies told to Parliament, bribery and stories sold to the newspapers. Lord Denning's superbly written report into the scandal describes with astonishment and fascinated revulsion the extraordinary sexual behaviour of the ruling classes. Orgies, naked bathing, sado-masochistic gatherings of the great and good and ministers and judges cavorting in masks are all uncovered.

ISBN 0 11 702402 3   Price £6.99

The Judgement of Nuremberg, 1946

"Efficient and enduring intimidation can only be achieved either by Capital Punishment or by measures by which the relatives of the criminal and the population do not know the fate of the criminal. This aim is achieved when the criminal is transferred to Germany."

The Backdrop

WWII is over, there is a climate of jubilation and optimism as the Allies look to rebuilding Europe for the future but the perpetrators of Nazi War crimes have still to be reckoned with, and the full extent of their atrocities is as yet widely unknown.

The Book

Today, we have lived with the full knowledge of the extent of Nazi atrocities for over half a century and yet they still retain their power to shock. Imagine what it was like as they were being revealed in the full extent of their horror for the first time. In this book the judges at the Nuremberg Trials take it in turn to describe the indictments handed down to the defendants and their crimes. The entire history, purpose and method of the Nazi party since its foundation in 1918 is revealed and described in chilling detail.

ISBN 0 11 702406 6   Price £6.99

The Boer War 1900: Ladysmith and Mafeking

"4th February – From General Sir Redvers Buller to Field-Marshal Lord Roberts … I have today received your letter of 26 January. White keeps a stiff upper lip, but some of those under him are desponding. He calculates he has now 7000 effectives. They are eating their horses and have very little else. He expects to be attacked in force this week … "

The Backdrop
The Boer War is often regarded as one of the first truly modern wars, as the British Army, using traditional tactics, came close to being defeated by a Boer force which deployed what was almost a guerrilla strategy in punishing terrain.

The Book
Within weeks of the outbreak of fighting in South Africa, two sections of the British Army were besieged at Ladysmith and Mafeking. Beginning with despatches describing the losses suffered by the British Army at Spion Kop on its way to rescue the garrison at Ladysmith, the book goes on to describe the lifting of the siege. The second part of the book gives Lord Baden Powell's account of the siege of Mafeking and how the soldiers and civilians coped with the inevitable hardship.

ISBN 0 11 702408 2   Price £6.99